ALL ABOUT K-POP

Inside Stories behind K-pop's Rise to Global Fandom

by Annika Chung

CHP

Coal Harbour Publishing

All About K-Pop. Inside Stories Behind K-pop's Rise to Global Fandom.

125A-1030 Denman St. Vancouver,
British Columbia, V6G 2M6, Canada
www.coalharbourpublishing.com

Publication Data

Author: Chung, Annika
Title: All about K-pop. Inside Stories Behind K-pop's Rise to Global Fandom /Chung, Annika--1st ed.
Publication date: October 2018
Publisher: Coal Harbour Publishing Ltd.

ISBN 978-1-989043-26-4 (E-book)

ISBN 978-1-989043-25-7 (Paperback)

CHP

Table of Contents

CHAPTER 1

K-Pop takes to the Global Stage!

Over the last two decades, K-pop has gradually grown from South Korea's national pop music to a unique genre of global music with millions of fans around the world. From BTS to EXO and Big Bang, many K-pop acts enjoy global fandoms who have been passionately promoting K-pop in numerous ways. When BTS, South Korea's five-member boyband, took the No 1 spot on Billboard's World Album chart in early 2018, K-pop's global influence was no longer unnoticeable. Mainstream media in North America and Europe started reporting about K-pop with dramatic headlines like "How K-pop conquered the world" (Rolling Stone August 21, 2018) and "How K-pop became a global phenomenon" (Vox, February 26, 2018). For millions of K-pop fans, the global success of BTS did not come as a surprise. The rise of K-pop to the global stage has been in the making for two decades.

Did you know that since Billboard's Fan Army Face-Off first started in 2014, K-pop fandoms have been winning in four consecutive years? The Fan Face-Off (Billboard's annual battle of global fandoms) has been dominated by K-pop fans. The fandom of Korean boy band, Big Bang, was the winner in 2014 and the fandom of Korean girl band, T-ara, took the top spot for the next three years. In 2018, the fandom of Korean boyband, Super Junior, became the winner (SBS Pop Asia, 30 August 2018).

At numerous times, K-pop acts have gained international recognition by having their albums or singles on the American

Billboard chart 100. Ever since the South Korean girl band, Wonder Girls, made it to the American Billboard Hot 100 chart in 2009, several South Korean acts followed suit. Given that American mainstream media do not regularly play K-pop, that was quite an astonishing achievement for K-pop acts. In 2018, BTS' single "Fake Love" ranked No 10 on America's Billboard Hot 100 while holding the first spot on iTunes' top selling album chart in 73 countries (Guardian, 5 June 2018).

BTS at a press conference for the Billboard Music Awards in 2017
(Photo Credit: TenAsia)

Aside from international music charts, K-pop's growing popularity has been reflected in the record number of YouTube views of K-pop music videos (MVs). Psy's MV, "Gangnam Style," received more than *3 billion* views on YouTube (Romano, 2018). Although Psy was not able to capture global attention after this viral video, many K-pop artists have shown that K-pop is not just a temporary fad. As table 1.1 shows, many K-pop hits have garnered more than 10 million views within the first 24 hours after the MVs were posted on YouTube. Music videos of many K-pop acts (such as BTS, Twice, Black Pink, and Big Bang in particular) are extremely popular on YouTube. The girl group Twice's "Likey" and "TT" gained more than 100 million views on YouTube in 36 days after its release (Romano, 2018). BTS' "DNA" hit more than 20 million views on YouTube in just 20 hours (CNN, 20 September 2017), while BTS' "Fake Love" attracted 35.9 million views within the first 24 hours (Straits Times, 4 June 2018). As of September 2018, BTS' DNA received 509 million views, while Big Bang's single, "Fantastic Baby", garnered 364 million views. The enormous popularity of K-pop led YouTube to create a specific K-pop entry to its existing musical entries in 2012 (Messerlin, 2017).

Table 1.1 The top 10 most viewed K-pop music videos **within the first 24 hours** as of May 2018. (Source: DatJoeDoe 2018)

Rank	MV title/ K-pop act (Year of Release)	The Number of Views
1	"Gentleman" by PSY (2013)	38.4 million
2	"Fake Love" by BTS (2018)	35.9 million
3	"DNA" by BTS (2017)	20.9 million
4	"Mic Drop" by BTS (2017)	13.9 million
5	"As If It's Your Last" by Black Pink (2017)	13.3 million
6	"What is Love?" by TWICE (2018)	12.5 million
7	"Daydream" by J-Hope (2018)	12.1 million
8	"Heart Shaker" by TWICE (2017)	11 million
9	"Not Today" by BTS (2017)	10.9 million

10	"Likey" by TWICE (2017)	10.7 million

As K-pop's presence on the Internet and video-sharing platforms such as YouTube continue to grow, K-pop related search results on the Internet in multiple languages have skyrocketed. The number of K-pop-related Web sites on the Internet is constantly on the rise. For instance, as of 2010, a search for "K-pop" on Google produced over 86 million results in English; 2,100,000 results in Indonesian; 2,200,000 results in Thai; and 3,100,000 results in Vietnamese (Jung 2011). Eight years later, in July 2018, a google search for K-pop provided 1, 820 million results in English. This is about 21 times more results compared to those 8 years ago!

K-pop is more than just a style of music. It is a cultural phenomenon as it inspires transnational fan communities to get involved in a diverse array of creative and collaborative activities including cover dance, fanfiction, and charity work. K-pop, together with other Korean cultural products such as K-dramas and TV shows, has given rise to KCON, the massive Korean cultural conventions, where K-pop concerts and exhibitions of various cultural products (TV drama, cuisine and cosmetics) are held around the world. KCON features concerts, workshops, panels and fan meetings attended by hundreds and thousands of K-pop fans. KCON has been held in various countries including France, Mexico, Japan, the USA and the UAE (Financial Times, 23 August 2017). In 2017, KCON LA, which took place in Los Angeles, drew 128,000 participants (Brown 2018). The highlight of KCON was a K-pop music concert which featured many K-pop groups including GOT7, SEVENTEEN, and WANNA ONE.

As shown, K-pop has emerged as a distinct genre of music and a global cultural phenomenon. Yet, it is only recently that the media outlets in the English-speaking world have begun to pay due attention to K-pop. How can we explain K-pop's rise to global fandom? To answer this question, this book grapples with the following questions.

What is the secret of K-pop's global appeal? Chapter 2 explores attractive characteristics of K-pop which are distinctive from other types of pop music. Who are the most popular K-pop groups in South Korea? Chapter 3 provides key information about the top 10 most popular K-pop acts in South Korea. It also briefly touches on popular solo artists and IndiMusic bands. Who are the most popular K-pop acts outside South Korea? Are there differences in K-pop fans' preferences depending on countries? How do you measure popularity? Chapter 4 explores regional variations and measurement issues regarding the popularity of K-pop acts outside South Korea.

What do K-pop's Transnational Fan communities look like? Chapter 5 examines K-pop fandoms around the world and provides a brief profile of K-pop fan clubs. What do K-pop fans do to promote their favorite artists? Chapter 6 discusses a wide range of fan activities including cover dance, random dance challenge, fan fiction, and charity work, among many others.

Chapters 7 and 8 address questions concerning the K-pop industry and the system of music production. What is K-pop and how did it develop? Chapter 7 explores a history of South Korea's pop music from the 1990s to the present. It provides a brief summary of major K-pop acts in the last two decades. Who are the major players in South Korea's music industry? What does the making of K-pop entail? Chapter 8 examines major label companies and their innovative approaches to music production. It explores diverse areas of music production including composition, choreography, MV directing, recruiting and training potential K-pop artists.

The remaining chapters (9-11) discuss the K-pop phenomenon through sociological lenses. They examine the following questions.

What is the relationship between K-pop and “Hallyu” (the Korean Wave)? K-pop is said to have led the Second Korean Wave. The First Korean Wave, which began in the mid-1990s, was largely led by Korean TV dramas. Chapter 9 discusses characteristics of the First and the Second Korean Wave and explores the role of K-pop in spreading Hallyu beyond Asia. Aside from innovative music companies and dedicated fandoms, what other factors played a role in creating societal environments conducive to the development of K-pop? Chapter 10 examines the role of politics, businesses, and culture in the development of K-pop. Some K-pop critics argue that K-pop artists largely lack musicianship and that they are just trained by corporations as export products. Others assert that K-pop is popular due to its “cultural hybridization” by incorporating “Western” cultural elements into Korean music. Chapter 11 discusses cultural biases embedded in some narratives around K-pop. It seeks to debunk some myths behind the juxtaposing perspective of “Western” versus non-Western culture that still influences the way many people think about K-pop.

CHAPTER 2

The Secret behind K-pop's Global Appeal

People unfamiliar with K-pop are likely to wonder why K-pop attracts millions of people around the world, who don't even understand Korean lyrics. How does K-pop transcend linguistic barriers? What is the secret behind K-pop's global appeal? This chapter explores musical and artistic characteristics of K-pop that are attractive to millions of people around the globe. They include:

Experimental and highly syncretized music
Catchy refrain with addictive beats
Amazing choreography and signature dance
Cool and colorful music videos
Multi-talented performing artists

In the following, each characteristic will be explained with some examples.

Experimental and Highly Syncretized music

It is not so much lyrical contents but the sound that first and foremost attracts people. Think about classical music or instrumental jazz music. Without vocal components, the sound of instruments can emotionally move people. The same principle applies to K-pop's global success. It is the beat, the sound, and the melody that makes K-pop so popular.

K-pop is a highly syncretized music drawing on a variety of music style including hip-hop, rap, EDM, R&B, and ballad. Syncretizing various genres of music, K-pop composers experiment with diverse sound tracks and melodies to create songs attractive to people across cultures. In other words, K-pop is not just a hybrid fusion music but, in fact, a distinct genre of music that creatively amalgamates diverse musical elements.

Catchy Refrain with Addictive Beats

Even if a sound track is attractive, people are less likely to cherish it, if it contains lyrical contents that are too controversial. Most K-pop's lyrical contents tend to be non-controversial as they focus on love, heartbreak or other themes that are universally applicable to people of all ages and cultures. This adds a broader appeal to K-pop since children and pre-teens can also enjoy it.

Furthermore, many K-pop fans note that K-pop's catchy refrain is one of K-pop's appeal. As an Indian woman from Delhi, comments, "Their music (K-pop) is so catchy and groovy. You can feel it" (Hindustan Times, 9 August 2017). Indeed, many K-Pop songs contain addictively catchy lines (Lie 2014). For example, some famous K-pop hits with catchy refrains include: "Gee" by Girl's Generation, "Nobody" by Wonder Girls, "Sorry, Sorry" & "Mr Simple" by Super Junior, "Mister" by Kara, and "Dope" and "Fire" by BTS, to name just a few.

Some of the catchy refrains are in English, which helps non-Korean listeners to sing along, but Korean refrains are equally abundant in K-pop. As shown at fan-gatherings and K-pop concerts abroad, a non-Korean audience does not seem to have any trouble with singing aloud catchy Korean refrains.

Amazing Choreography and Signature Dance

Many K-pop fans note that they are attracted to well-choreographed dance movements that accompany K-pop songs. They find that K-pop's dance moves are highly sophisticated and extremely well-synchronized. Some K-pop songs that are famous for their expertly conceived choreography include: "Wolf" by EXO, "Lucifer" by SHInee, "Fire" by BTS, and "Mirotic" by TVXQ, to name just a few.

EXO at 2013 K-pop World Festival in South Korea (Photo Credit: Korea.net)

Similar to catchy refrains, many K-pop groups perform certain dance moves that are unique to each individual song, in a repetitive but highly choreographed manner. Let's take Super Junior's "Sorry Sorry" as an example. The repetitive "signature dance" consists of a series of gestures such as the hand-rubbing and finger-snapping as well as the cross-armed circular movements. A K-pop analyst has likened signature dance moves associated with certain K-pop songs to "kinetic equivalents of lyrical refrains" (Lie 2014). As a result, most K-pop songs get additional names associated with their own signature dance. For instance, the "crab dance" is associated with Girls' Generations' "Gee", the "butt dance" with KARA's "Mr," and the "Horse Dance" with Psy's "Gangnam Style" (Kim Y, 2013).

Cool and Colorful Music Video

Many K-pop fans have commented that they find K-pop music videos very attractive. K-pop's powerful appeal is not only in the superbly choreographed dance movements but also in the means (i.e. MVs on free social media) by which they are presented. For instance, the music video of Psy's "Gangnam style" attracted more than 3 billion views on YouTube alone, although mainstream media outside South Korea did not play Psy's song until his MV went viral.

The popularity of K-pop can be easily detected if we look at the number of views that they attract on YouTube alone. As of September 2018, BTS's "DNA" scored almost 500 million views. Twice's "TT" got 400 million views, while Black Pink's MV "As if it's your last" received 398 million views. Other K-pop music videos attracting nearly 400 million views include BTS' "Dope" (361m views) and Black Pink's "Boombayah" (373m views) and Psy's "Daddy" (372 m views). The number of views accounts only for official MVs on YouTube. If we include the viewership on other video sharing sites such as Youku and others, the number will be easily well over one billion, far higher than the figure in table 2.1.

Table 2. 1 Selected list of Official K-pop MVs with over 300 million views on YouTube (as of September 2018)

K-pop Act	MVs (Views of Official K-pop MVs)
BTS	DNA (498,993,457 views) MIC Drop (340,100,484 views) Blood Sweat & Tears (351,201,834 views) Fake Love (319,696,181 views) Dope (361,929,769 views)
Psy	Daddy (372,825,024 views) Gentleman (1,190,134,050 views) Gangnam Style (3,212,445,383 views)
Black Pink	Boombayah (373,952,121 views) DDU-DU DDU-DU (364,840,457 views) As if it's your last (398,269,168 views)
Big Bang	Fantastic Baby (363,543,074 views) Bang Bang Bang (329,379,369 views)
Twice	TT (400,545,621 views)

Multi-talented but Relatable K-pop Artists

K-pop's popularity owes a great deal to performing artists who are extremely multi-talented. It is not just the song that matters only. Who sings the song decisively matters in the fandom-driven K-pop world. Some may argue that K-pop performers' good-look is related to their popularity but their stylish appearance alone, however, cannot sustain their fandom in the long run. In South Korea's highly competitive music industry, many K-pop artists also work as composers, lyricists, and even actors, and/or TV show hosts. For many K-pop fans, artists' musicianship is what has attracted them to their favorite stars. In an interview with Billboard, Colette Bennett, a 40- year-old writer from Atlanta, gives a reason why he likes K-pop and BTS, a Korean boyband, in particular. As he put it:

> BTS appealed to me for the same reason BIGBANG did during my intro to K-pop in 2011. K-pop was always fun music to me that I enjoyed. When I discovered BIGBANG, the biggest thing that impressed me the most was that they wrote their own music and it was often more than just "Hey, let's go party." They were kind of setting a precedent and BTS, you know, they were huge BIGBANG fans and I feel like they carry that torch. BTS are in a good place where they're making music that is both catchy and that people want to listen to and dance to but they're also making music that they're communicating through. (Billboard, 29 September 2017)

In addition to musicianship, K-pop artists are loved by their fans because of their relatable public persona. Most K-pop artists regularly appear in TV variety shows where they show off their multi-talents and reveal their life stories. This contributes to the likeability of K-pop artists. Asked about the appeal of K-pop, Thai fans answered that they like K-pop because they feel closer to their stars, almost like K-pop stars are their close old friends, after learning about stars daily life through TV reality shows (KOFICE, 29 January 2018). As a K-pop fan from India also put it: "You watch the K-pop idols on variety shows and know about their life stories. They are so hard working, it gives me patience, I get inspiration from them" (Hindustan Times, 9 August 2017).

CHAPTER 3

Most Popular K-pop Acts: An Overview

South Korea is blessed with many talented K-pop artists. Since K-pop emerged in the early 1990s, hundreds of K-pop acts have appeared. While some disappeared from the public eye, many still produce hits that are widely popular. Very popular K-pop acts such as Big Bang, SHINee, and Girls' Generation have been around more than 10 years, while others have debuted only in the early 2010s. Although some K-pop acts including 2NE1 and Kara have disbanded, individual artists of the disbanded groups continue to perform as soloist.

Table 3.1 Selected List of Popular K-Pop artists since 2000 (in alphabetical order)

AOA, 2AM, A-Pink, After School, B1A4, Big Bang, Block B, Boyfriend, Black Pink, Brown Eyed Girls, BTS, B2ST (Highlight), Cosmic Girls, CLC, C.N. Blue, Code-V, Dalmatian, DIA, Epik High, EXID, 4 Minute, F.T. Island, F(x), Girls Dream Catcher, Day, GFriend, Gavy NJ, Got 7, Infinite, iKon, I.O.I., IU, JYJ, KARA, KARD, KNK, MBLAQ, Miss A, Monsta X, NUEST W, NCTU, NCT 127, 2NE1, N-Train, Orange Caramel, Pentagon, Pristin, 2PM, Rain, Red Velvet, Rainbow, Seventeen, Se7en, Secret, SNSD (Girls' Generation), SHINee, SISTAR, SM the Ballad, SS501, Super Junior, T-ara, Teen Top, TVXQ, U-Kiss, Wonder Girls, Twice, Triple H, Wanna One, WEKI MEKI, Winner, VIXX

This chapter provides an overview of the most popular K-pop acts in the last 5 years. It should be noted that K-pop acts' popularity vary significantly depending on a number of factors. Such variables may include: country, age, the method of measuring popularity, gender, and time, among many others. Regional variations in the popularity of K-pop acts and the difficulty of measuring popularity will be discussed in detail in the next chapter.

Taken into consideration the difficulty of gathering accurate data representative of a global audience, this chapter has selected only a handful number of K-pop acts for an overview of their achievements. The K-pop acts mentioned in this chapter have frequently appeared in the media and SNSs across countries in the last five years.

Among many popular K-pop groups (see table 3.1), the top 10 most popular K-pop bands across regions may include the following acts: BTS, EXO, Big Bang, Super Junior, Got 7, Girls' Generation (SNSD), Infinite, TVXQ, SHINee and Twice. In the below, a brief profile of each group will be followed by their notable achievements.

BTS

BTS, a seven-member boy band, was formed by Big Hit Entertainment in 2013. BTS is an acronym for *Bangtan Sonyeondan* (방탄소년단) which means "bulletproof boys" in English. RM and Suga, two BTS members, were underground rappers before they joined BTS. All BTS members participate in the production of their music. In particular, RM, Suga and J-Hope have written the lyrics of many BTS songs which reflected their personal experience of hardship and challenges that they face in their pursuit for music.

Bangtan Boys in Hongdae (Photo Credit: Taehyung's Moment)

RM, the leader of BTS, mostly speaks for the group at international venues since he is the only one in the group who can speak English fluently. In an interview, he said that he learned English by watching American sitcoms such as "Friends". Suga, the lead rapper of BTS, has his stage name deriving from the two syllables of "Shooting Guard" for he loves basketball. Lead singer Jungkook, joined BTS when he was 15 years old (Benjamin 2017). The handsome vocalist, V (real name Kim Tae-hyung), is also an actor. He starred in several Korean dramas including *Hwarang*.

Table 3.2 BTS Members: A Profile

Member	Profile
RM (Rap Monster)	Position: Group leader, Main rapper Birth Year: 1994 Real Name: Kim Nam-joon (김남준)
J-Hope	Position: Lead Rapper, Main Dancer Birth Year: 1994 Real Name: Jung Ho-seok (정호석)
Jimin	Position: Lead Vocalist, Main Dancer Birth Year: 1995 Real Name: Park Ji-min (박지민)
Jungkook	Position: Main Vocalist, Lead Dancer Birth Year: 1997 Real Name: Jeon Jung-gook (전정국)
Jin	Position: Vocalist Birth Year: 1992 Real Name: Kim Seok-jin (김석진)
Suga	Position: Lead Rapper Birth Year: 1993 Real Name: Min Yoon-gi (민윤기)
V (브이)	Position: Vocalist Birth Year: 1995 Real Name: Kim Tae-hyung (김태형)

Since their debut in 2013, BTS has released several albums. Some of their best-known singles include:

> Boy in Luv (2014), No More Dreams (2014), War of Hormone (2014), I need U (2015), Run (2015), Dope (2015), Blood, Sweat & Tear (2015), Fire (2016), Save

Me (2016), DNA (2017), MIC Drop (2017), Fake Love (2018), Idol (2018)

In contrast to some K-pop acts with cheerful Bubblegum pop style, BTS music is considered to have more depth and meaning. BTS has tackled social issues like depression, anxiety, and loneliness in their songs. Their earlier songs, in particular, have dealt with issues that Korean youth faced. They critiqued the negative impacts of South Korea's competitive education on youths.

BTS' rise to global fame has been gradual. In 2015, two years after their debut, BTS had their song, "I Need U," on Top 10 hit in South Korea. In 2016, BTS' album *Wings* became Korea's best-selling album of the year with pre-orders for the album reaching over 500,000 copies within the first week (Benjamin 2017). By 2016, BTS made inroads into other Asian music markets. As BTS produces a Japanese version of their songs, their Japanese album, *Blood Sweat & Tears* topped the Japan Hot 100 chart (Benjamin 2017). BTS was awarded the Mnet Asian Music Award for Artists of the Year in 2016 and 2017.

By 2017, BTS' popularity reached a global stage as BTS's songs hit the Billboard Hot 100. Responding to the growing demands from international fans, BTS performed global concert tours. BTS' American tours in 2017 was a huge success. As tickets for BTS concerts in the USA were sold out within minutes, two more concerts were added due to strong demands from their fans. In the same year, BTS won the Top Social Artist position at the Billboard Music Award (Benjamin 2017). The boyband remained for 31 weeks at the top of *Billboard*'s Social 50 chart, which is an international ranking of the most popular singers around the world (Benjamin 2017).

BTS's popularity on social media is unprecedented. In 2017, BTS became the most tweeted music group in the world by earning a

Guinness World Record of 502 million tweets. It was reported that they were tweeted far more than any other celebrities in the world. In 2017, *Time* magazine included BTS as one of its "25 Most Influential People on the Internet" list (Huffington Post, 2017). By 2018, BTS' s Twitter account has more than 16.5 million followers, BTS appeared on the 2018 *Forbes* list which features the 300 most influential young people in Asia (Forbes 2018). Although not selected as one of TIME 100, BTS gained 15% of the Reader Poll votes, beating everyone on the list (Benjamin 2017).

In 2018, BTS became the first K-pop act to hit No. 1 on the *Billboard* Artist 100 chart. BTS's single "Fake Love" received more than 35.9 million views on YouTube within 24 hours after its release and reached 100 million views in just eight days (Forbes, May 26, 2018). BTS has about 10 million Korean followers on their V live TV (Korea's popular video-sharing app) channel alone.

Big Bang

Big Bang, a five-member boy band, was formed by YG Entertainment in 2006. As in the case with BTS, Big Bang members all take part in the production of their songs. While all Big Bang members are well-established songwriters, G-Dragon and T.O.P. in particular, have composed and written many hits. For instance, G-Dragon has composed his own singles including *Lies* (2007), and *Last Farewell* (2007). T.O.P has written several Big Bang hits including *Loser* (2015) and *Bang Bang Bang* (2015). Aside from their group activities, all members have a successful solo career. Taeyang wrote the lyrics of his solo hit, *Eyes, Nose, Lips* (2014), while Seungri produced his solo hit, *What can I do* (2012). Daesung has also produced his own albums.

Big Bang members (Photo credit: LGE 2010)

Big Bang has produced numerous hits. Their best-known singles are as follows:

> We Belong Together (2006), La La La (2006), Shake It (2007), Lies (2007), Always (2007), Last Farewell (2007), Day by Day (2008), Sunset Glow (2008), Lollipop (2009), Tonight (2011), Love Song (2011), Blue (2012), Fantastic Baby (2012), Monster (2012), Ringa Ringa (2014), Loser (2015), Bae Bae (2015), Let's Not Fall In Love (2015), Last Dance (2016), Bad Boy (2016), Bang Bang Bang (2016), Zutter (2016), Sober (2016), We like 2 party (2016), Crooked (2016), and Good Boy (2017)

Starting with the Song of the Year Mnet music award for Big Bang's song *Lies* in 2007, the group has received many music awards from both domestic and international establishments. Big Bang won the Best Worldwide Act award from the 2011 MTV Europe Music Awards. The boy band took the Best Asian Artist award at the 2018 Japan Gold Disc Awards.

Big Bang's two albums, *Alive* and *MADE*, made it to the Billboard 200 chart (Billboard, 13 March 2018). Big Bang's first global concert tour took place in 2012 in major cities in four continents. Over 550,000 international fans came to Big Bang's global concerts in 2012. Big Bang's second world tour took place in 15 countries between 2015 and 2016. In 2016, almost two million fans in China alone tried to buy tickets for Big Bang's 10th anniversary concert in Seoul. That meant that they were planning to fly to South Korea just to attend Big Bang's concert (South China Morning Post, 2 March 2018). Big Bang is also hugely popular in Japan. Almost one million people attended Big Bang's concerts in Japan between 2015 and 2016 (Forbes June 18, 2018). In 2017, 50,000-tickets for Big Bang's concert in Tokyo were completely sold out (Jolin 2017).

Table 3.3 Big Bang Members: Profile

Member	Profile
GD (G-Dragon)	Real name: Kwon, Ji-yong Birth Year: 1988 Position: Leader, Rapper, Vocalist
Taeyang	Real Name: Dong, Young-bae Birth year: 1988 Position: Main Vocalist, Main Dancer
T.O.P	Real Name: Choi, Seung-hyun Birth Year: 1987 Position: Lead Rapper
Seungri	Position: Vocalist, Lead Dancer

	Real Name: Lee, Seung-hyun Other Stage Name: also known as "V.I" in Japan Birth year: 1990
Daesung	Real name: Kang, Dae-sung Other stage name: "D-Lite" in Japan Birth year: 1989 Position: Vocalist

All Big Bang members are very popular TV personalities. They have frequently appeared on many TV variety shows including *Family Outing*, *Running Man, Infinite Challenge*, and *Knowing Brothers*. In addition to Korean TV programs, Seungri, who is fluent in Japanese, has also often appeared on Japanese TV variety shows. The main rapper of the band, T.O.P., is an actor. He has played a leading role in several films including *Tazza; The Hidden Card*, *Commitment*, *Iris*, and *Out of Control.* As of August 2018, Big Bang has 10.5 million followers on Facebook.

EXO

The group's name, EXO, refers to an *exo*planet that exists outside of the solar system. EXO was originally a 12-member boy band that was formed by S.M Entertainment in 2011. EXO was initially divided into two subgroups, EXO-K (South Korea) and EXO-M (China). Over contractual disputes with SM Entertainment, three members of EXO-M (Kris, Luhan, and Tao) left the band between 2014 and 2015. As a result, EXO-M disbanded and the remaining members joined the current EXO, which now consists of nine members. They are: Suho (the group leader), Baekhyun, Chanyeol, D.O., Kai, Sehun, Xiumin, Lay, and Chen. The three former members of EXO-M continue their music career as soloist in China.

EXO at Mnet Asian Music Awards in 2014 (Photo credit: Tochanyeol)

Since their debut single "Mama" was released in 2012, EXO produced numerous hits. Their best-known singles include:

> Wolf (2013), Growl (2013), Call me baby (2015), Love me right (2015), Monster (2016), Dancing King (2016), Power (2017), The Eve (2017), Ko Ko Bop (2017)

EXO's single "Growl" was an enormous success in 2013 since their first album sold over one million copies. EXO won the Album of the Year at the Mnet Asian Music Awards (MAMA) in 2013 and received the Artist of the Year and "Album of the Year" awards at the 2014 MAMA. EXO's single "Wolf" charted No. 3 on Billboard's K-pop Hot 100 in 2013 (Soompi January 17, 2015). In 2014, EXO was awarded the "Most Popular Asian Group" and

"Asia's Best Performance" awards at the 2014 "Youku Night" in China. Every year, the "YOUKU Night" selects the most popular MVs based on the number of views and fan votes (Soompi January 17, 2015). EXO has won over 88 music program awards between 2014 and 2015 (Mare-Sensei 2017). The band ranked first in the most influential celebrity category by Forbes Korea Power Celebrity during the same period (Mare-Sensei 2017).

Albeit less known than BTS on global stage, EXO has a huge fanbase in Asia. EXO performed live at the Closing Ceremony of the PyeongChang 2018 Winter Olympic Games that took place in South Korea. As of 2018, EXO has 7.5 million followers on Facebook and 6 million on Korea's V Live, 3.4 million on Instagram, and 4.5 million on China's Weibo.

EXO members at Seoul Music Awards in 2015. (Photo credit: Xing comma Hun)

Most EXO members have appeared on Korean movies and TV dramas. Ximin was featured in the movie “Seondal: The Man Who Sells the River” (2016), while Baekhyun played a junior role in the Korean TV drama, “Moon Lovers: Scarlet Heart Ryeo” (2016). The most successful actor among the multi-talented EXO members is D.O. (real name Do Kyung Soo). D.O. has starred in numerous films and TV dramas including “Along with the Gods: The Two Worlds” (2017), “Room No.7” (2017), “Swing Kids” (2018), “It’s Ok, This is Love” (2014), and “100 Days My Prince” (2018) (Kprofiles 2018).

Super Junior

Along with Big Bang, Super Junior is one of the older K-pop groups that have been around more than a decade. Super Junior (also known as SuJu) was initially a 13-member boy band formed by SM Entertainment in 2005. For various reasons, the group has been reduced to nine members as of 2018. The current Super Junior members include: Ye-sung, Kyu-hyun, Siwon, Ki-bum, Han-kyung, Sung-min, Dong-hae, Hee-chul, Eun-hyuk, Lee-teuk, Kang-in, Reyo-wook, and Shin-dong.

Super Junior at the 1st Asia Tour Concert in 2008. (Photo credit: SM Entertainment)

As in the case with EXO, Super Junior had a Chinese sub-unit, Super Junior-M. After two Chinese members (Han Geng and Henry Lau) left the SM label company between 2008 and 2009, the Chinese unit remains inactive. Kyu-hyun, Ye-sung and Ryeo-wook are part of Super Junior K.R.Y., a subunit, mainly focusing on R&B and ballad songs. A SuJu member, Shin-dong, is known to be responsible for the groups' choreography.

Super Junior produced numerous hits. Some best-known songs include:

> Sorry, Sorry (2009), It's You (2009), Bonamana (2010), Mr. Simple (2011), Spy (2012), Mamacita (2014), Super Girl (2015), Marry U (2015), Black Suit (2017), Lo Siento (2018)

Super Junior gained fame in Asia with its single "Sorry Sorry" in 2009. The song was so popular in Asia that numerous cover dance videos surfaced on YouTube. One of them was a video recording of some prisoners in the Philippines dancing to the tune of "Sorry Sorry" during their exercise hours. The cover dance video showing the prisoners' dance received over 4.6 million views at that time (Jung, 2011). By 2010, Super Junior was ranked as the number one worldwide trending topic on the Twitter weekly chart (Jung, 2011).

By 2012, Super Junior has gained recognition in Europe and North America as the band was nominated for "Best Asian Act" at the MTV Europe Music Awards. In 2014, Super Junior's album Mamacita became No. 1 on Billboard's World Album chart. Super Junior received thirteen music awards from the Mnet Asian Music Awards. At the end of 2014, Super Junior performed more than 100 concerts worldwide. In 2015, they won the "International Artist" and "Best Fandom" in the Teen Choice Awards (Allkpop 12 August 2015).

Super Junior's new single, "Lo Siento", released in 2018, became a mega hit in Latin America. For the first time in K-pop history, Super Junior became the first Korean act to be listed on Billboard's Latin Digital Song Sales chart. "Lo Siento" ranked at No.2 on the World Digital Song Sales Chart (SBS PopAsia 26 April 2018).

As in the case with most K-pop bands, many of the Super Junior members appear regularly in TV dramas, films and TV variety shows. They even hosted their own weekly variety show, *Super Junior's Super TV* (Herman, 15 July 2018). In addition, Hee-chul hosts a popular TV variety show, "Knowing Brothers". Si-won maintains a successful career as an actor. He played a leading role in numerous TV dramas including "Oh! My Lady" (2010), "Poseidon" (2011), "She Was Pretty" (2015), and "Revolutionary Love" (2017).

Super Junior has a strong, dedicated fanbase, called ELF (Everlasting Friends). In 2015, E.L.F won the award for the "Best Fandom" at the Teen Choice Awards. Thanks to E.L.F, Super Junior took the top spot on Billboard's Fan Army Face-Off in 2018, by receiving over 2 million votes, while the fans for Harry Styles garnered 1.8 million votes (Ilmare42, 2018).

Infinite

Infinite, a 7-member boy band, was formed by a smaller label company, Woollim Entertainment, in 2010. After one member (Hoya) left the group in 2017, Infinite currently has six members. They are: Kim Sung-Gyu (leader), Jang Dong-woo, Nam Woo-hyun, Lee Sung-yeol, Kim Myung-soo (known as L), and Lee Sung-jong. Aside from their group activities, some members of Infinite such as Sung-kyu and Woo-hyun also perform as soloist.

In 2011, Infinite's single, "Be Mine", won the top place at M! Countdown. In 2012, Infinite's song, "The Chaser", was chosen by Billboard as the number one K-Pop song of the year. In 2013, their album "New Challenge" became one of the best-selling albums of the year in South Korea. In 2014, Infinite's "Last Romeo", was ranked at the 33rd place on Billboard Twitter Top Tracks (Mare-Sensei 2017). By 2016, the band produced 15 albums and over 20 singles in both Korean and Japanese languages (Billboard, June 9, 2016).

Infinite has produced many hits. They include:

> Come Back Again (2010), Be mine (2011), Paradise (2011), The Chaser (2012), Destiny (2013), Last Romeo (2014), Back (2014), Nothing's Over (2015), Dilemma (2015), Bad (2015), and the Eye (2016).

Infinite Members (Photo credit: How to love 2015)

Some Infinite members pursue an acting career. Sung-yeol played a role in a TV drama, “Hi! School: Love On” (2014). Woo-hyun also starred in many TV drams including “Cheer Up On Love” (2009), “Jolly Widows” (2009-2010), “While You Were Sleeping” (2011), “D-Day” (2015). Likewise, Myung-soo regularly appeared in many TV dramas including “Master’s Sun” (2013), “Cunning Single Lady” (2014), “My Lovely Girl” (2014), “The Time We Were Not In Love” (2015), and “Ruler: Master of the Mask ” (2017).

Girls’ Generation (SNSD)

Girl’s Generation (aka SNSD from *So-Nyeo-Si-Dae* in Korean) is a girl band that was formed by SM Entertainment in 2007. The group initially consisted of eight members but currently has only five members: Taeyeon, Sunny, Hyoyeon, Yuri, and Yoona. In 2004,

Jessica left the group and Tiffany, Sooyoung, and Seohyun decided not to renew their contract with SM in 2017. SNSD's ex-members, Tiffany and Seohyun perform as soloist. While maintaining SNSD group activities, Taeyeon (the leader of the band) also performs as soloist and has produced several albums of her own.

Girls' Generation at KBS Music Awards (Photo credit: Pabian)

SNSD has produced numerous hits. They include:

> Run Devil Run (2010), Tell me your wish (2010), Gee (2010), Chocolate love (2010), Intro the New World (2007), The boys (2011), Mr. Taxi (2011), I got a boy (2013), Oh (2013), Girls (2015), Catch me if you can (2015), Party (2015), Holiday (2017), All Night (2017)

SNSD's "Tell Me Your Wish (Genie)" won the 2011 Record of the Year at the Golden Disc Awards in South Korea. The MV for "Genie" received the Best Group Video award at the MTV Music Awards in Japan. SNSD has many music videos that went viral on YouTube. For instance, "Gee" received 215 million views, while "The Boys" scored 203 million views. As a recognition of SNSD's huge popularity on YouTube, the group received the Video of the Year at the YouTube Music Awards in 2013 (Benjamin 2013).

Some SNSD members have starred in TV dramas and movies. For instance, Seo-hyun played a role in the TV drama, "Moon Lovers: Scarlet Heart Ryeo." Yoo-na has also starred in many TV drama series including "You are my destiny" (2008), "Love Rain" (2012), "Prime Minister & I" (2013), "The K2" (2016), and "The King in Love" (2017).

SNSD has a huge fanbase in China. Due to SNSD's huge popularity in China, Yoo-na also appeared in Chinese drama "God of War", while Jessica, ex-member of SNSD, starred in a Chinese film "I Love That Crazy Little Thing" (SBS PopAsia, 10 November 2017). Girls' Generation was the only Korean act invited to perform on China's CCTV's "New Year's Gala" in 2016 (SBS PopAsia, 10 November 2017).

TVXQ (DBSK)

TVXQ (also known as DBSK in South Korea) is one of the older K-pop groups that have been around more than a decade. TVXQ was initially a five-member boy band formed by SM Entertainment in 2003. The band split into two groups, TVXQ and JYJ in 2010. Currently, TVXQ has only two members, Yun-ho and Chang-min, while, JYJ, a split group formed by three ex-members, is with C-JeS Entertainment.

Chang-min and Yun-ho (Photo credit: Kamilie)

TVXQ produced many hits and some of their best known singles include:

> Hug (2004), The Way U Are (2004), Tonight (2005), Rising Sun (2005), Show me your love (2005), Balloons (2006), Mirrotic (2008), Wrong Number (2008), Keep your head down (2011), Before U go (2011), Catch Me (2012), Humanoids (2012), Something (2014), Spellbound (2014), The Chance of Love (2018)

Yun-ho (also known as U-Know) and Chang-min (also known as Max) are fluent in Japanese. They released over 50 Japanese singles, far more than their singles in Korean language (Forbes June 18, 2018). In 2008, TVXQ became the first Korean male act to take the top spot on the weekly Oricon chart, the Japanese equivalent of the

U.S. *Billboard* singles chart (Forbes June 18, 2018). Known as *Tohoshinki* in Japanese, TVXQ is enormously popular in Japan and has a huge fanbase with its own name, "BigEast". For all other countries except Japan, "Cassiopeia" is TVXQ's official fandom name (Forbes June 18, 2018). Between November 2017 and June 2018, close to one million Japanese people attended TVXQ's concerts which began in November 2017. With the record number of attendees, TVXQ became the first foreign music group to have most concertgoers at a single tour in Japan (Soompi, June 10, 2018).

Yun-ho is also an actor, starring in many K-dramas and films. He played a major role in several K-dramas including "Meloholic" (2017), "I Order You" (2015), "Night Watchman's Journal" (2014) and "Queen of Ambition" (2013).

SHINee

SHInee is a boy band created by SM Entertainment in 2008. The name "Shinee" derives from the combination of two words, English "shine" and Korean "ee (이 meaning a person)" (Mare-Sensei 2017). The group initially consisted of five members but after Jong-hyun, the group's leading vocalist and singer-songwriter, committed suicide in 2018, it has now only four-members. They are: Lee Jin-ki (Onew) (leader), Choi Min-ho, Kim Ki-bum (known as Key), and Lee Tae-min.

SHINee has produced numerous hits. Some of them include:

> Nuna is so pretty-Replay (2008), Ring Ding Dong (2009), Hello (2010), Lucifer (2010), Why so serious? (2013), Your number (2016), Tell me what to do (2016), Our Page, I want you, You & I, View (2015), Good Evening (2018)

SHINee (Photo credit: Kamilie)

In 2009, Shinee's single, "Ring Ding Dong" topped several Korean music charts. Over the last decade, the group's popularity expanded to Asia and Europe. The group's single, "Lucifer", was nominated for the Best Dance Performance Award at the Mnet Asian Music Awards in 2010 (Mare-Sensei 2017). As SHINee became popular, the band's album "Sherlock" ranked at the 6th place on the Swedish iTunes list in 2012.

SHINee's late Jong-hyun wrote, composed, and arranged many songs and albums for the group. Performing as soloist, he also produced his own albums. Some of the songs, that Jong-hyun helped to produce, include: Juliette (2008), Up & Down (2010), and Obsession (2010) (Danica 2018).

Aside from the group activity, Min-ho from Shinee maintains a very successful career as actor and song-writer. He starred in numerous TV dramas and movies. To name just a few, he played a leading role in: "To the Beautiful You (2012)", "The most beautiful goodbye"

(2017), "Somehow 18" (2017), "Hwarang" (2016), and "Because it's the first time" (2015). He is also a lyricist and wrote many songs including "Alarm clock", "Aside", "Beautiful", "Can't leave," and "Dream Girl".

GOT7

Got7 is a boy group that debuted in 2014 under JYP Entertainment. Like many other K-pop groups, Got 7 is a multinational band including performers from China (Hong Kong), Thailand, and the USA. The members of GOT7 include: JB (Im Jae-bum), Mark (Mark Yi En Tuan), Jackson (Wang Ka Yee), Jr Jinyoung (Park Jin-young), Youngjae (Choi Young-jae), Bam Bam (Kunpimook Bhuwakul), and Yugyeom (Kim Yu-gyeom).

GOT 7 Members (Photo credit: Ten Asia 2015)

GOT 7 has produced many hits. They include:

> Just Right (2016), Never Ever (2017), Hard Carry (2016), If you do (2015), Look (2018), You are (2017), Stop Stop It (2014), The New Era (2018), Confession Song (2015), Teen Ager (2017)

In 2014, Got 7's single "Stop Stop It" ranked at No. 4 on Billboard's World Digital Songs chart. In 2016, they won the Best Worldwide Act at the MTV Europe Music Awards.

As in the case with most popular K-pop artists, the band members are multi-talented. Jackson, the Got7 member from Hong Kong, won two gold medals in Asian fencing games. Mark from the USA has starred in a TV drama, "Dream High". Bambam, from Thailand, has also played a role in several movies in his home country.

TWICE

Twice is a multinational girl group formed by JYP in 2015. It comprises of nine women from South Korea, Japan, and Taiwan. The group members include: Na-yeon, Jeong-yeon, Momo, Sana, Ji-hyo, Mina, Da-hyun, Chae-young, and Tzuyu. Among the seven members, Momo, Mina and Sana are Japanese, while Tzuyu, is Taiwanese. Twice consisted of the final winners of the 2015 reality K-pop competition show, *Sixteen*, from which only seven contestants out of 16 were chosen (Herman, 27 October 2016).

Twice (Photo credit: News in Star)

Although Twice is a relatively new K-pop act, they have already produced numerous hits. They include:

> TT (2016), What is love? (2018), Likey (2017), Heart Shaker (2017), Dance the night away (2017), Candy Pop (2018), Knock Knock (2017), Signal (2017), Like Oh Ah (2015), I want you back (2018), Cheer Up (2016), One more time (2017)

Twice's debut album ranked at No. 15 of *Billboard*'s World Albums chart in 2015 and one year after, their second album took the No. 6 spot (Herman, 27 October 2016). Twice's music style is known to be Bubblegum pop, exemplified in their mega hits, "TT" and "Cheer up". In 2016, Twice's single, "Cheer Up," became the fastest K-pop video to attract more than 50 million views on YouTube in less than two months. In 2018, TWICE's single "Likey", received well over 300 million views on YouTube.

Like TVXQ and Big Bang, the girl group Twice is very popular in Japan. In 2017, Twice won the Oricon Queen Award, which is given to the most popular female celebrities in Japan (Peterson, 2017). TWICE also won the Song of the Year Award at the 2017 Mnet Asian Music Awards (MAMA).

Other Popular K-pop Acts: From iKon, and Red Velvet to Black Pink

Many other K-pop acts enjoy huge popularity in Asia and beyond. They include: iKon, Black Pink, Red Velvet, Teen Top, and Block B, to name just a few. Table 3.4 shows some examples of popular K-pop bands with their hits.

Table 3.4 Other Popular K-pop Bands and their hits

K-pop Act	Hits
Block B	Yesterday (2017), Shall we dance (2017), Her (2014), Nillili Mambo (2012), Nanrina (2012)
Teen Top	Rocking (2013), Supa Luv (2011), Love is (2017), Alone (2014), To you (2012), I'm sorry (2014)
Black Pink	Boombayah (2016), Playing with fire (2016), Stay (2016), DDU-DU DDU-DU
Red Velvet	Bad Boy (2017), Dumb Dumb, Red Flavor (2017), Peek-A-boo (2017), Russian Roulette (2016)
B.A.P	One shot, No Mercy (2012), Stop It (2012), Hurricane (2013), Honeymoon (2017), Wake me up (2017), Hands Up (2017)
iKON	Love Scenario (2018), Bling Bling (2017), Dumb & Dumber (2015), Anthem (2015), What's wrong (2015), Rhythm Ta (2015), Apology (2015), Airplane (2015)

Seventeen	Very nice (2016), Clap (2017), Don't wanna cry (2017), Cal call call (2018), Boom boom (2016), Adore U (2015), Thanks (2018)
Akdong Musician	Give Love (2014), Dinosaur (2017), Last Goodbye (2017)
EXID	DDD (2017), Up & Down, Hot Pink (2016), Night Rather Than Day,
Wanna One	Energetic (2017), Boomerang (2018), Burn it up (2017), Pick me (2017)
2NE1*	I'm the best (2011), Come back home (2014), Lonely (2011), Falling in love (2014), Let's go party (2011), Good bye (2017)
B2ST (Highlight)	Fiction (2011), Beautiful (2011), Beautiful Night (2012)
4Minute*	First (2010), What's your name (2013), Whacha' doin' today (2014)
f(x)	Hot Summer (2011), La cha Ta (2011), 4 Walls (2015), Chu (2011), Pinocchio (2011)
MBLAQ	Stay (2011), Be a Man (2014), Cry (2011), Mirror (2015), Good Luv (2010), Oh Yeah (2011), This is War (2012), Smokey Girl (2013), Mona Lisa (2011), Y (2011)
C.N.Blue	Intuition (2011), Between Us (2017), Let's go crazy, Love, I'm sorry, One Time
Kara*	Mama Mia (2015), AHA (2007), Go go summer (2011), Step (2011), If U Wanna (2007), We are with you (2010)
2 A.M	This song (2010), Like a fool (2010), Over the destiny (2014), One day (2012), One Spring Day (2013), I love you (2010)
2 P.M	My house (2015), Heartbeat (2009), I'm your man (2011), Hands Up (2011), Go Crazy (2014), Without you (2011), I'll be back (2011)
Apink	I'm So Sick, Mr Ch (2014), NoNoNo (2015), Bubibu (2012), I don't know (2015),
NCT 127	Cherry Bomb (2017), Chain (2018), Limitless (2017), Fire Truck (2016)

Momoland	Bboom Bboom (2018), Baam (2018), Wonderful love (2018), Freeze (2017)

* Disbanded

As for relatively new boybands, iKon has emerged as one of the most popular boy groups in South Korea. iKon is a 7-member boy band formed in 2015 by YG Entertainment. The group produced many hits including "Love Scenario" (2018) and "Rhythm Ta" (2015). B.I, the group's rapper, is a successful songwriter and record producer. He has produced numerous hits for the group as well as for other artists. As of 2018, iKon's official YouTube channel has about 3.4 million subscribers (see table 4.5).

Among girl groups, Black Pink, Red Velvet, and T-ara have seen their popularity fast rising in many parts of the world. Black Pink is very popular on many video portal sites such as YouTube. Black Pink's MV "DDU-DU DDU-DU" attracted more than 379,7 million views in just three months after it was released on YouTube. Even just a reaction video of Black Pink's "DDU-DU DDU-DU" gained over 1.4 million views within two months after it was uploaded on YouTube (Hi Chad, July 24, 2018).

Red Velvet, debuted under SM Entertainment in 2014, is a girl group rapidly gaining some global attention. Their album "Perfect Velvet" topped the Billboard World Albums Chart in 2017 and their next album "Summer Magic" topped the iTunes Albums chart in 28 regions in 2018 (Straits Times Aug 31, 2018).

Red Velvet (Photo credit: HeyDay)

In recent years, T-ara has became one of the most popular K-pop girl groups in China. The music video for T-ara's single "Little Apple" gained over 8 million views within one day after it was released on the Chinese video site Youku (KpopStarz November 26, 2014). Among all Korean girl groups, T-ara has the largest fan club in China. With 2.3 million fans in 2018, T-ara has surpasses SNSD that has 2.6 million registered fans in China (KBIZOOM March 2018).

Popular K-pop Solo Artists: From IU, and Zico to Zion T.

K-pop is not all about multi-member, same-gender groups that sing catchy songs and perform dynamic and synchronized dance movements. Aside from popular K-pop bands, many more K-pop artists perform as soloist with diverse repertoires of music genre ranging from R&B and ballade to rap.

While most solo artists have been always solo, others debuted as soloist while maintaining their group activities or after their bands disbanded. For instance, Psy, IU, BoA, and Ailee have always been solo, while G-Dragon and Taeyang have maintained both their solo and group activities. In most cases, as table 3.5 shows, many individual members of the currently active K-pop groups also perform as soloist.

Table 3.5 Popular Solo Artists (affiliated K-pop group)

IU., Zion. T, Crush, Rain, BoA, Ailee, Psy, Heize, K.Will, CL (2NE1), Taeyeon (Girls' Generation), Sunmi (Wonder Girls), G-Dragon (Big Bang), T.O.P (Big Bang), Taeyang (Big Bang), Dean, HyunA (4 Minute), Holland, Jessi, Reowook (Super Junior), Taemin (SHINee), Baek-hyun (EXO), Jay Park, Zico (Block B), Henry (Super Junior-M), Kyu-hyun (Super Junior), Yesung (Super Junior), Bobby (iKon), Hyolin (Sistar), Chungha, Yoon Jong-sin, Yoon Sang, Wheesung, Lee Seung-hwan, Shaun, Roy Kim, Park Hyo-sin, Hwang Chi-yeol, Im Chang-jeong, Kim Bum-soo, Kim Gun-mo, Eric Nam, Samuel, Lee Tae-min, Minji, Soyou

Among the popular soloists, IU stands out. As table 4.1 in the next chapter shows, she ranked No. 1 of South Korea's most popular K-pop artists of the year in 2014 and 2017, while taking the No. 2 spot in 2015. It is not BTS nor Big Bang, when it comes to the most beloved singer among people across all age groups in South Korea. She is also equally popular in China. With more than 1.5 million registered fans in China alone, IU is immensely popular among Chinese people (KBIZOOM March 2018). Although she is less known to listeners in Europe and the Americas, she has tremendous potential to appeal to a broader audience outside Asia. As a successful singer-songwriter, actor, and music producer, she has produced numerous hits including “The Red Shoes (2013)”, “Twenty-three (2015)”, “Friday (2013)”, “Good Day (2010)”, “Palette (2017)”, and “Dear Name (2017)”.

IU (photo credit: Yoon Min-hoo)

As for popular male soloists, Zion.T, Zico, and K.Will have maintained steady popularity in South Korea. They stand out with their unique style of music incorporating ballad, R&B and rap. Like IU, all three soloists are prolific songwriters and music producers, helping to create numerous hits. Zion.T 's hits include: "Yanghwa Brdg (2013)", "Baby (2013)", "No Make up (2015), and "Snow (2017)". Zico (a member of the boyband Block B) has composed and written many songs. Some of his best-known singles include: "Okey Dokey (2016)", "I am You, you are me (2016)", "Bermuda Triangle (2016)," "Artists (2017)", and "Soulmate (2018)".

Zion T, Crush, and Zico at KCON 2015. (Photo credit: Mduangdara)

K.Will's best know songs include: "I need you (2012)", "You don't know (2013)", "Please, don't know (2012)", "Eat (2015)","Talk Love (2016), and "Day 1 (2014)". In 2012, his single, "I Need You", ranked at No. 2 on the Billboard K-Pop Hot 100 and in the same year, he received the Mnet Asian Music Award for Best Vocal Performance.

CHAPTER 4

Popularity Variation across Nations and Social Media

Popularity varies depending on where listeners live and how their preferences are measured. In addition, demographic factors such as age and gender also play a role. This chapter analyzes variations in the popularity of K-pop artists across countries and different social media platforms. First, it outlines dominant social media platforms across regions and how they affect the ranking of popularity. Second, it identifies the most popular K-pop artists across YouTube, Twitter, and Facebook, that are all available in most countries, except a few countries including China. Third, it explores how international rankings are different from South Korean preferences for K-pop artists. The South Korean example is followed by a discussion of variations in K-pop popularity in China that uses different SNS tools (Weibo, Youku, and Baidu).

Assessing popularity of K-pop on different Social Media Platforms

K-pop's popularity on social media significantly varies depending on countries. Although the number of views that K-pop MVs garner on YouTube may be an indicator for popularity in some countries, YouTube viewership does not represent people in China or Iran where such SNS tools are not available. Likewise, Twitter and Facebook might provide information on the popularity of K-pop acts in some countries but do not include people who use only their own national SNS tools such as Naver, Vline, Weibo, and Youku, to name just a few.

Albeit almost all social media platforms run by US companies are available in South Korea, many Koreans still heavily use their domestic SNS tools including Naver, Daum, Vline, and Kakao Talk. Almost all, smartphone users in South Korea use Kakao Talk instead of WhatsApp or Snapchat. Similarly, Japanese people also use, albeit less heavily, their own domestic apps in addition to using American ones. In contrast, Chinese people exclusively use their own domestic equivalents such as Baidu, Youku, and Weibo, since most American SNS tools (Google, YouTube, and Facebook) are not available in China.

Given so many multi-platforms used in different countries, it is quite a challenging task to gather accurate global data on the number of K-pop fan communities and the number of regular users on SNS across nations.

Table 4. 1 Various Social Media Platforms in the USA, South Korea, and China

	The USA	Korea	China	Japan
Search Engine & Webhosting	Google Yahoo	Naver, Google, Daum	Baidu	Yahoo!, Google
Video sharing	YouTube/ VMO	YouTube, Vline, Kakao TV	Youku	YouTube, Viki
Blogging	Facebook, Twitter, Instagram	Facebook, Twitter, Kakao Story, Naver Band, Daum	Weibo	Ameba, Pixity

Messaging	Snapchat, Whatsapp, Messenger	Kakao Talk, Whatsapp, Snapchat, Messenger	WeChat	Line/ IOS

Popular K-pop Artists on YouTube and Twitter across all Regions except China

Since YouTube, Twitter, and Facebook are widely used in most countries around the world, user trends on the US-based SNS platforms show some important information about the popularity of K-pop acts worldwide. This section, however, only focuses on YouTube and Twitter. The information about K-pop artists' popularity on Facebook will be discussed in the next chapter in conjunction with K-pop fan clubs.

Table 4.2 K-pop Acts' Official YouTube Channels and the number of subscribers as of September 20, 2018

	Official YouTube Channel of K-pop Act	Subscribers
1	BLACKPINK	12 million
2	BTS	11,6 million
3	Big Bang	10 million
4	iKON	3,4 million
5	Twice	2,8 million
6	GIRLS' GENERATION	1,7 million
7	EXO	1,7 million
8	G-DRAGON	1,2 million
9	SUPER JUNIOR	966,695

10	SHINee	913,512
11	TVXQ	326,986

As table 4.2 shows, about 9 K-pop acts have more than one million subscribers on their official YouTube channel. Black Pink has the largest number of subscribers (12 million), closely followed by BTS (11.6 million) and Big Bang (10 million). Five other K-pop acts on the list that have between 3 and 1 million subscribers are: iKon (3.4 million), Twice (2.8 million), SNSD (1.7 million), EXO (1.7 million) and Super Junior (1 million).

According to the user trends on Twitter, however, BTS seems to be the most popular K-pop act. As for Twitter, BTS surpasses all other K-pop acts. BTS's Official Japan Twitter account alone has 4.2 million followers, while its Korean Twitter and its official English Twitter have 16.5 million and 12.4 million followers respectively as of September 2018. It is a stark contrast to other big K-pop acts. For instance, Big Bang's official global Twitter account in English has 1.58 million followers as of September 2018. Another example is IU, the most popular singer among South Koreans. According to IU's official Twitter, she has only 67,000 followers.

As mentioned earlier, the information based on US-run SNS tools should be supplemented with the information of users of national SNS platforms. For instance, if we look at Big Bang's account on Weibo, the Chinese version of Twitter, the number of Big Bang followers (7.2 million) exceeds BTS' (3,3 million), as shown in table 4.7. In addition, since a language barrier fragments the use of Twitter and Facebook, it is rather difficult to get accurate information about users' preferences.

Popular K-pop Artists in South Korea

When it comes to identifying the most popular K-pop acts in South Korea, it is relatively easy since Korea Gallup conducts an annual survey of the popularity rating of K-pop artists based on different age groups.

According to Korea Gallup, the most popular K-pop artist in 2017 is IU, a singer-songwriter, by garnering 15.2% votes. Since the result was based on a survey of Koreans between 13 and 59 years old, it is clear that IU is loved by Koreans across all age groups. Twice, a girl group, took the second spot, while the world-renowned boyband, BTS, who is very popular in North America, ranked only No. 4.

Table 4.3 Top-10 most popular K-pop stars among Koreans (aged between 13 and 59) in 2017 (Source: Korea Gallup 2017)

Rank	K-pop Artists	Percentage
1	IU	15.2%
2	TWICE	9.1%
3	Jang Yoon-jeong	8.9%
4	BTS	8.5%
5	Yoon Jong-sin	7.3%
6	Wanna One	7.1%
7	EXO	5.7%
8	Big Bang	5%
9	Im Chang-jeong	5%
10	Lee Sun-hee	4.6%

K-pop artists' popularity varies over time. Some K-pop acts such as SNSD, which topped the survey charts between 2009 and 2011, did not make it to the top-10 popular list of 2017. Similarly, Big Bang which topped the chart in 2015 ranked only at No.8 in 2017. Instead, newer groups such as BTS, Twice, and Wanna One have been gaining popularity among South Koreans. The rise and fall of K-pop acts in terms of popularity can be seen in table 4.2 which shows the most popular K-pop artists among South Koreans between 2007 and 2016.

Table 4.4 From 2007 until 2016: The top-5 most popular Korean singers among Koreans aged between 13 and 59. (Source: Korea Gallup 2017)

Rank	2007	2008	2009	2010
1	Wonder Girls (29.2%)	Wonder Girls (22.2%)	SNSD (29.8%)	SNSD (31.5%)
2	Big Bang (16.8%)	Big Bang (21.2%)	Big Bang (21.1)	2PM (12.5%)
3	Jang Yoon-jeong	Jang Yoon-jeong	2PM	Jang Yoon-jeong
4	SNSD	SNSD	Wonder Girls	Tae Jin-ah
5	SG Wanna B	Lee Hyo-ri	Jang Yoon-jeong	Kara

	2011	2012	2013	2014
1	SNSD (26.1)	Psy (24.4)	Jo Yong-pil (17.6)	IU (12.9)
2	Big Bang (8.2)	SNSD (19.8)	Psy (11.7)	SNSD (12.4)
3	Jang Yoon-jeong	Big Bang (9.5)	Jang Yoon-jeong	Sistra
4	Kim Bum-su	IU (6.9)	EXO	EXO
5	IU	Jang Yoon-jeong	SNSD	Lee Sun-hee

Rank	2015	2016	2017	
1	Big Bang (15.5%)	Im Chang-jeong (11.8%)	IU	
2	IU (15.4)	Twice (9.9)	Twice	
3	SNSD	Jang Yoon-jeong	Jang Yoon-jeong	

4	Jang Yoon-jeomg	EXO	BTS	
5	Sistra	SNSD	Yoon Jong-sin	

Although most top-five positions have been occupied by well-known K-pop acts such as SNSD, Big Bang and EXO, it is interesting to note that Jang Yoon-jeong has almost consistently made it to the top-5 popular list. Known as the queen of South Korea's traditional trot music, she is not really considered a typical K-pop star. The main reason that she is listed on the top-5 is her popularity among older generations of Koreans. Similarly, ballad singers such as Yoon Jong-sin, Kim Bum-soo and Im Chang-jeong are very popular among older generations of Koreans.

Indeed, the age variable significantly affects a popularity rating. Table 4.5 shows the top-10 most popular singers among younger generations of Koreans aged between 13 and 29. The survey results reveal some interesting information about younger South Korean's music preferences. As table 4.3 shows, there is no trot singer on the chart but only K-pop artists. IU is still very popular as she ranked either No. 1 or No. 2 on the list. This clearly shows that many younger Koreans also love R&B and Soul style music that IU performs. Big Bang has been consistently listed on the top-5. Other K-pop acts popular among younger Koreans include: SNSD, Twice, APink, EXO, Miss A, Wanna ONe, Block B, and BTS.

Table 4.5 From 2015 until 2017: Top-10 most popular K-pop artists among younger Koreans (aged between 13 and 29). (Source: Korea Gallup 2017)

Rank	2015	2016	2017
1	IU (21.5%)	SNSD's Taeyon (11.8)	IU (14.5%)

2	Big Bang's G-Dragon (15.8%)	IU (6.6)	Wanna One's Gang Daniel (9)
3	SNSD's Taeyon (11.7%)	TWICE's Tzuyu (6.3%)	Big Bang G-Dragon (7.9)
4	Big Bang's Taeyang (7.7%)	Big Bang's G-Drago (5.9)n	Red Velvet's Irene (6.4)
5	Sistra's Hyorin (6.9%)	EXO's Chan-yeol (4.5)	Big Bang's Taeyang (6.3)
6	APink's Jeong Eun-ji (5.7%)	APink's Jeong Eun-ji (4.4)	Twice's Nayeon (6)
7	EXID's Hanni (5.5%)	Sistra's Hyorin (4.3)	BTS's Jimin (5.7)
8	SNSD's Yoo-na (5.2%)	EXO's Baekhyun (3.7)	Block B's Zico (5.4)
9	EXO's Chan-yeol (5.1%)	Big Bang's Taeyang (3.7)	AOA's Seolhyun (3.8)
10	Miss A's Suzy & AOA's Seol-hyeon (4.7%)	AOA's Seol-hyun (3.6)	SNSD's Taeyon & Twice Tzuyu (3.8)

As to the popularity of K-pop acts outside South Korea, it is difficult to gather accurate data, given that there is no national survey similar to the Korean one. Popularity can be measured in multiple ways. Some indicators of popularity include: the ranking on national music charts, the sale of CDs and online streaming, the number of registered fan club and fan-cafe members, subscribers and followers of K-pop artists' SNS platforms, among many other factors.

Popular K-pop Artists on Weibo, Baidu, and Youku in China

One of the most popular social media platforms in China is Weibo, Chinese microblogging website, which has more than 431 million active users as of 2018. China's Weibo works like American twitter. By using hashtags, Weibo users can easily organize and identify topics and posts. As of May 2018, according to Weibo Hashtag list (see table 4.6), the top 3 K-pop acts with the most views include: EXO, BTS, and Big Bang. EXO received close to 49 million views, while BTS and Big Bang got close to 33 million and 31 million views respectively (Allkpop May 2, 2018). The Weibo account of EXO's Sehun alone has almost 400,000 followers.

Table 4.6 Top-15 most popular K-pop acts on China's Weibo Hashtag (Source: Allkpop, May 2, 2018)

Rank	Group	Hashtag views
1	EXO	48.9 million
2	BTS	32.9 million
3	Big Bang	31.5 million
4	Got 7	20.5 million
5	Girls' Generation	17.4 million
6	Winner	12 million
7	iKon	7.6 million
8	Black Pink	6.4 million
9	Shinee	5.8 million
10	f(x)	5.5 million
11	Super Junior	5.37 million
12	Infinite	5.3 million
13	VIXX	5.2 million
14	TVXQ	5 million
15	Seventeen	4.7 million

EXO dominates in China as the most popular K-pop act. Weibo's PowerStar regularly ranks Korean pop stars in terms of popularity in China. As of April 2017, the 10 most popular Korean artists in China, according to Weibo's PowerStar, included: EXO's Sehun, Hwang Chi-yeol, EXO's Baekhyun, EXO's Chanyeol, Big Bang's G-Dragon, and f(x).

This finding is somewhat consistent with other SNS platforms such as Youku, with some variations depending on the time of survey. Begun in 2016, Youku is the Chinese version of YouTube, now owned by Alibaba Group. Youku is one of the biggest video platforms in China and has over 500 million monthly active users and 15 billion visitors per month (Chozan, 2017).

Table 4. 7 shows the most streamed Korean artists online on all platforms in China as of July 2018. EXO took the first spot with 4,5 billion times, followed by Big Bang (3,8 billion) and T-ara (1,9 billion), Girls' Generation (865 million), G-Dragon (448 million), Taeyon (417 million), Super Junior (363 million), F(x) (297 million), Shinee (243 million), and IU (197 million) (Allkpop (July 29, 2018). It is interesting to note that BTS has not been prominently featured on online streaming platforms in China. One may speculate that a Chinese boycott of Korean cultural contents since the end of 2016 (see chapter 9) might have hindered the viewing of BTS on such platforms. This does not mean that BTS is not popular as table 4.8 shows.

Table 4.7 The most streamed Korean artists online on all platforms in China (Source: Allkpop, July 29, 2018).

Rank	K-pop Act	Times
1	EXO	4,497 million
2	Big Bang	3,843 million
3	T-ara	1,9 68 million
4	Girls' Generation	865 million
5	G-Dragon	448 million
6	Taeyon	417 million
7	Super Junior	363 million
8	F(x)	297 million
9	Shinee	243 million
10	IU	197 million

If we look at K-pop fan cafes and fan clubs in China, however, the result is slightly different from the one based on online streaming. As of July 2018, the top 10 K-pop acts with the biggest fandom in China in terms of fan-cafe members are: EXO, T-ara, and Big Bang, Girls' Generation, Super Junior, TVXQ, f(x), SHINee, 2PM, and JYJ (Allkpop, July 29, 2018). Here again, BTS does not belong to the top-10.

Chinese Twitter, Weibo, provides some interesting information about new trends among Chinese K-pop fans. In terms of followers on K-pop artists' official Weibo, Big Bang has the largest numbers (7.2 million), followed by BTS (3.3 million).

Table 4.8 Official Fan clubs on Weibo and the number of followers as of 22 September 2018

Official Fan club on Chinese Weibo	Followers
EXO 中文网-exofan club	1,1 million
BTS	3,3 million
Big Bang Asia	7,2 million
Shinee	118,777
SNSD (少女时代中文首站)	1,4 million
Got 7	974,853
TWICE 吧官博	542,242
Super Junior	1,4 million
TVXQ	229,367

The number of fans belonging to fan clubs and fan-cafes is an important indicator for assessing K-pop's popularity. The next two chapters discuss the regional distribution of K-pop fan communities around the world in detail.

Chapter 5

Transnational K-pop Fandom

Many K-pop acts have massive transnational fan bases. Most typical forms of K-pop community exist as fan cafes or fan clubs. Some are officially endorsed by label companies, while a majority of fan cafes and fan clubs are run by fans themselves. One of the main differences between official fan cafes and official fan clubs is a membership fee. Fan cafes are free to join. The members of fan cafes regularly receive update news on K-pop artists from their label companies (Soompi, 20 January 2016). Except some label companies such as SM, most entertainment houses maintain official fan cafes for their artists on Daum or Naver (Korean equivalent of Google or Firefox). In addition, a countless number of unofficial fan cafes and fan clubs exist on various social media platforms such as Facebook and Amino.

Official fan clubs require an annual membership fee which can range between 8 and 25 US dollars (Soompi, 20 January 2016). The application fee for BTS' official fan club, ARMY, is around 7 US dollars (Karolina, 2016). The benefits of official fan club membership include: pre-reservations and priority ticket sales for concerts and fan meetings and access to exclusive photos and video clips (Karolina, 2016). In addition, members receive some goodies such as tote bags and the official light-stick as part of their membership.

Registering for official membership can be a challenge for many fans, since new members are accepted only once a year or very intermittently, and even then, only during a short time period, membership applications can be submitted (Soompi, 20 January 2016). Many K-pop groups accept new members to their fan club once a year, others such as SHINee's official Fan club (Shawol) do so irregularly.

Regulations concerning membership registration also vary depending on countries. Some official fan clubs or fan cafes accept only the residents of South Korea. The Official Japanese Fan club, Shinee World-J, requires a Japanese address, barring non-residents to join. TVXQ has two official fan clubs: Cassiopeia (Korea & International) and Big East (Japan). Due to language barriers and difficult registration requirements, many international fans find it hard to join official fan clubs. Against this backdrop, close to 6,000 Big Bang fans abroad signed a petition to ask YG Entertainment to accept iVips (Big Bang's unofficial fan club) as part of YG official fan club for Big Bang.

Aside from official fan clubs and fan cafes, numerous informal fan communities of all sizes exist not only on Facebook or Chinese Weibo, but other social media sites such as Band, Tumblr, Amino and Chinese Baidu. For instance, Amino App allows people to create and join communities of people with shared interests. To share information and news on K-pop acts, unofficial K-pop fan communities loosely exist across all social media platforms. This chapter identifies such fan communities across countries. First, it provides a brief overview of fan clubs for some popular K-pop acts. Then, it examines the status of some prominent fan communities in four regions: Asia, North America, the Middle East and Africa, Latin America, and Europe.

Official Fan Clubs and Fandom Names

All K-pop acts have their dedicated fan clubs at home but some K-pop groups such as BTS and Big Bang have massive fan bases abroad. As table 5.1 shows, K-pop fan clubs have their own unique names and colors representing the fan clubs.

Table 5.1 Top 10 K-pop bands and their fandom names & Color (Source: www. kprofiles.com)

K-Pop Group	Fandom Name
BTS	A.R.M.Y (Adorable Representative MC for Youth) Color: Silver Gray
Super Junior	ELF (Everlasting Friends) Colour: Pearl Sapphire Blue.
SNSD (Girls' Generation)	S♥NEs (pronounced "so ones", meaning that SNSD & their fans are one.) Colour: Pastel Rose.
Big Bang	V.I.P. = Very Important Person. Colour: yellow + black
Infinite	Inspirit Colour: Unknown
EXO	EXO-L Color: Cosmic Latte
TVXQ	Cassiopeia Colour: Pearl Red
SHINee	Shawols (Shining Land = SHINee + World) Colour: Pearlescent Sky Blue
TWICE	Once Color: Apricot & Magenta
GOT7	I GOT7 Color: Green and White

BTS's fandom, ARMY, stands for "Adorable Representative M.C for Youth". Given that BTS means Bangtan (Bullet Proof) boys, the fandom name, ARMY, complements the group.

The official fan club for EXO is called, "EXO-L" which stands for "EXO-Love." According to EXO-L website, the registered members reached over 4 million as of April 2017 (SBS PopAsia, 26 April 2017). When the EXO-L website first opened for membership application in 2014, it crashed due to too much online traffic by EXO fans who tried to register (Korea Herald, August 5, 2014).

Shinee's fandom, *Shawol*, derives from the combination of first syllables of two words, Shinee and World. *Shawol* means Shinee World. The official name for Big Bang's fan club is V.I.P. which stands for "very important person." Super Junior's fandom is called ELF which stands for "Everlasting Friends". The name of TVXQ's official fan club is Cassiopeia, a five star-constellation, which refers to the original 5 members of TVXQ before it split with JYJ.

Distribution of Fandoms by Regions

Let's look at the distribution and characteristics of K-pop fan communities (official fan clubs, fan cafes, and unofficial fan groups) in some selected countries by region.

Asia

As table 5.2 shows, K-pop acts with more than 7 million followers on Korean Facebook include: Big Bang, BTS, EXO, Super Junior, and Girls' Generation (SNSD). Big Bang has the highest number of followers on Korean Facebook, as it has more than 10 million followers.

Table 5.2 K-pop fan communities on Korean social networking sites such as Daum, Amino and Facebook (as of September 2018)

K-pop Act	SNS (Members / Followers)
BTS	Official BTS Daum Café (1,104,206) Official Facebook (7,628,417)
EXO	Official Facebook (7,566,272) Daum Café (115,132)
Super Junior	Official Facebook (7,654,136) Daum café—Chun Whee Ryong (97,940)
Infinite	Daum Café (204,141) Facebook (1,354,150)
Big Bang	Official Facebook (10,549,998) Official Big Bang Daum café (213,982)
Girls' Generation (SNSD)	Daum Café—HwaSuEubHwa (188,378) Facebook (7,062,308)
Shinee	Facebook (5,771,341) Daum–Heeinae Shinee Fan-cafe (75,184)
Twice	Daum Café (39,444) Official Facebook (2,265,344)
Got7	Daum fan-cafe (49,513) Amino Fan-cafe (174,760) Official Facebook (4,198,954)
Seventeen	Facebook (1,785,484)
MonstaX	Daum café (87,989) Facebook (1,283,084)
Black Pink	Official Facebook (2,453,031)
iKon	Official iKon Facebook (1,045,572)
Red Velvet	Facebook (1,146,497)
TVXQ	TVXQ! Facebook (1,760,308) Daum café—Yuaerubi (325,307)

Teen Top	Facebook (1,345,861)

China has by far the biggest K-pop fan clubs outside South Korea. Big Bang has more than 11 million official fan club members in China. The next top six K-pop acts with a massive fanbase in China are as follows: G-Dragon (6,7 million), EXO (4,6 million), SNSD (2,6 million), T-ARA (2,3 million), IU (1,5 million), and BTS (1,4 million) (KBIZOOM March 2018).

Now, when we look at fan-cafes in China (table 5.3), EXO still tops the top-10 most popular K-pop acts in China. T-ara and Big Bang are neck and neck for the second highest number of fan-cafe members.

Table 5.3 Top 10 most popular K-pop Acts in China in terms of their Chinese fan café members (Source: Allkpop July 29, 2018)

Rank	K-pop Act	No. of Chinese Fan cafe members
1	EXO	3.7 million
2	T-ara	2.5 million
3	Big Bang	2.3 million
4	SNSD	1.9 million
5	Super Junior	1.4 32,774
6	TVXQ	1.432,546
7	f(x)	894,666
8	Shinee	893,900
9	2PM	788, 612
10	JYJ	695,645

As table 5.2 shows, F(x)'s fan café in China has 2.5 million members. f(x) is popular in China due to Victoria, a Chinese member in the girl group. Victoria alone has over 10 million followers on her Weibo (Chinese Twitter) site.

Japan has the second biggest K-pop fan club bases after China. Numerous K-pop fan clubs in Japan have more than 10,000 fans who pay regular membership fees. In terms of only the paying members (as of July 2018), the top five K-pop fan clubs in Japan include: TVXQ (530,000), SHINee (310,000), Big Bang (290,000), BTS (260,000), and EXO (160,000) (Allkpop, 4 July 2018).

K-pop's popularity extends beyond Japan and China. It has a huge following in Southeast Asia including India, Indonesia, Malaysia, the Philippines, and Vietnam.

EXO has a fairy big fan base in India (Gogoi 2017). As of 2017, EXO had over five thousand members in India according to its official fan club, EXO-L India (Gogoi 2017). The Bangtan ARMY India, which was formed in 2014, claims about 2,300 ARMY members as of July 2017 (Gogoi 2017).

According to the Philippine Kpop Committee Inc. (PKCI), it represents 60 local K-pop fan clubs. Indonesia's national organization of K-pop fans, "United K-pop Lovers Indonesia (UKLI)", claimed about 48,000 members as of 2011.

In Malaysia, Big Bang is very popular. As a Malaysian online blogger reported, the Malaysian Big Bang fan club had a rented bus covered with Big Bang photos and ads about the group's concert in 2015 (see figure 5.1).

Super Junior is very popular in Thailand. The "SuperJunior Thai ELF," an unofficial fan club in Thailand, has more than 81,000 followers on Facebook and about 30,000 active members, as of January 2018 (KOFICE, 29 January 2018).

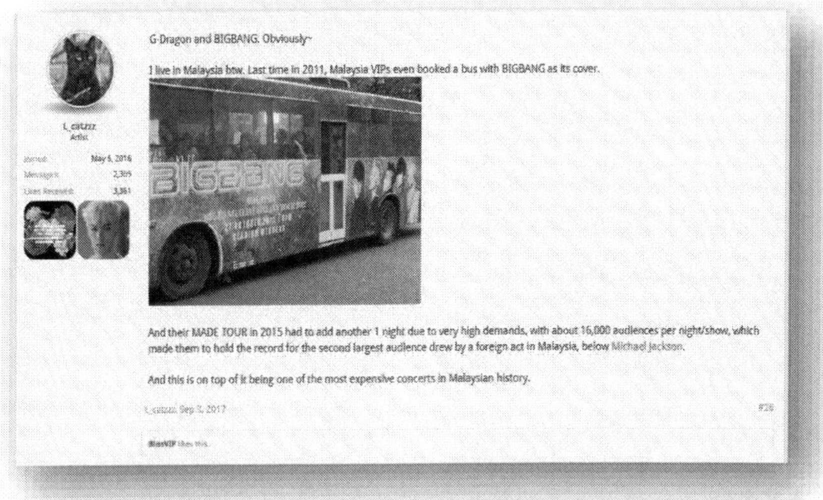

Figure 5.1 Big Bang Fan Bus in Malaysia. (Allkpop 3 September 2017. FireShot Capture)

North America

All major K-pop acts have sizable fanbases in North America. In particular, BTS, Big Bang, TVXQ, and SHinee are very popular in North America.

North America has hundreds of informal BTS fan groups. For instance, ARMY Amino (aka ARA) is an informal BTS fan community on Amino. ARA claims more than 1.4 million members as of September 2018 (ARA, 21 September 2018). Mainly operating in English speaking countries, "BTS Fambases" is another informal community made of 100 BTS fan clubs and has about 104,000 followers. "US BTS ARMY" is another example of a US-based BTS fan community that is not affiliated with BTS' management company, Big Hit Entertainment.

Figure 5.2 Twitter page of "BTS Fambases" (FireShot Capture)

Other K-pop acts such as TVXQ and SHINEee have sizable fanbases in North America. "WE ARE T" is an informal US-based, international fan club for TVXQ. Using English as lingua franca, it represents international fans who could not have a voice with SM due to some difficulties (language barriers and registration requirements) of accessing official fan clubs (Cassiopeia and Big East). Formed in 2012, "We Are T", claims about 30,000 registered members on its website and 7,600 members on Facebook as of August 2016 (My Music Taste, August 26, 2016). Likewise, "Shinee USA" is an unofficial fan club based in the USA. It claims about 3,400 followers on Facebook and 2,500 on Twitter.

The Middle East and Africa

Several informal K-pop fan groups with hundreds and thousands of members exist in the region. They include "Kpop Arab", the "Crazy K-pop Fans" and "The SM Family World". In Palestine, the "Kpop Palestine" claimed about 1,500 members in 2014. The SM Family

World, as of 2013, claimed more than 33 million visitors to its Facebook site, including more than 12,000 followers from the Palestinian Territories, 7,331 from Israel, and over two million from Saudi Arabia (Otmazgin and Lyan, 2014).

In 2013, about 103 online Facebook communities, dedicated to 103 K-pop bands, existed in Israel (Otmazgin and Lyan, 2014). As of 2014, the biggest K-pop fan organization in Israel was "South Korean Lovers" which claimed more than a thousand members (Otmazgin and Lyan, 2014). Super Junior, SHINee, Big Bang, BTS and EXO are very popular in the Middle East and North Africa. Most K-pop fan communities have a couple of hundred members. For instance, Big Bang's unofficial fan club in Israel, "BIGBANG Israel", has 472 members, while "EXO Israel" has 360 followers as of 2018.

Figure 5.3 K-pop fans in Egypt

(Photo credit: Korean Culture and Information Service)

Several BTS fan communities share news on BTS and promote BTS music on Twitter. One of the fan groups, "Egyptian 방탄 ARMY" on Twitter has more than 6,000 followers, while another group, "Bts Egypt" has about 1,200 followers as of September 2018.

BTS is also very popular in the United Arab Emirate (UAE). A BTS fan club in the UAE, "BTS UAE ARMY", has almost 7,000 followers on Facebook, while 30,000 people follow "BTS UAE" on Twitter as of September 2018.

Latin America

Most big K-pop acts including Super Junior, SNSD, EXO, BTS, and Big Bang have fairly big fan bases in South America. Many fan communities operate via Facebook and Twitter.

For instance, "Bangtan Brasil", BTS' fan community in Brazil, has 256,000 followers on Twitter, while an informal BTS fan community in Brazil, "BTS É O FLUXO" has about 111,000 followers on Facebook as of 2018. A Brazilian fan club for Super Junior, "Super Junior Brasil (E.L.F)", has more than 30,000 followers, while another Super Junior fan club, "SuJu Brasil" has more than 12,000 followers on Facebook as of September 2018.

EXO is also popular in Brazil. An informal EXO fan community, "EXO Brasil", has more than 44,000 followers on Facebook in 2018. Other EXO fan groups in Brazil, "EXO Planet BR" and "EXO MEMES BR" have about 45,000 followers and almost 12,000 followers respectively on their Facebook as of September 2018. Table 5.4 provides examples of fan communities in just a few countries in Latin America.

Table 5. 4 Latin American K-pop fan communities on Facebook (followers as of September 2018)

Country	Fan Groups (No. of Followers)
Mexico	BTS México Alianza Latina (171,028) EXO Latinoamérica (91,586) EXO México (51, 185) The EXO'rdium MX (25, 902) Big Bang Mexico (55,045) BIGBang México (17,446)
Brazil	BTS É O FLUXO" (110,849) Super Junior Brasil (E.L.F) (30,308) SuJu Brasil (12,362) EXO Brasil (44,156) EXO Planet BR (44,916) EXO MEMES BR (11,512)
Argentina	ELF Argentina (24,643) Super Junior-Argentina (ELF Latinas) (4,487) BTS Army's Argentina (22,056) Bangtan Boys Argentina FC (1,773) Rise on Bangtan Argentina (27,717) Big Bang Argentina "My Heaven" (15,643) Got7 Argentina Official (39,832) MonstaX Argentina (24,478)
Perú	BTS 방탄소년단 – Perú (99,623) BTS ICA- Perú (1,915) Super Junior Perú (38,558) EXO Peru (70,043) EXO Perú (6,497) D.O. Perú (42,266) Lay Perú (18,022) SNSD Perú Fan club-SONES Perú (20,404) Seohyeon Perú (21, 186)
Chile	BTS Chile (109,636) ARMY Chile (42,267) Super Junior Chile (11,361) Super Junior (E.L.F Chile) (1,231) Got 7 Chile (39,152) Girls Generation Chile (16,400) Black Pink Chile (14, 296) Kai We ARE EXO Chile (7,741)

	EXO Fans Chile (2,253)

In Peru, the boyband EXO is very popular. As table 5.4 shows, two members of EXO, D.O. and Lay in particular, have a sizable fanbase in Peru. By 2014, Mexico reportedly had about 70 K-pop fan clubs (Choi et. al., 2014). An informal BTS fan club, "BTS México Alianza Latina", has 171,028 followers on Facebook in 2018. EXO and Big Bang also have sizable fanbases in Mexico.

Europe

In 2012, Norway had about 69 fan communities active via Facebook (Antonsen 2012). "Kpop Norge", established in 2011, was the largest K-pop fan community in Norway with 1,630 members in 2014 (Rånes 2014). In 2013, there were reportedly about fifty online active K-Pop fan communities in Romania (Marinescu and Balica, 2013).

"KpopEurope" is an informal network of K-pop fans in Europe. By operating in 13 different languages of European countries (German, French, Italian, etc.), the KpopEurope aims to bring together K-pop fans across Europe. According to "K-popEurope", more than 200 K-pop fan clubs existed in Europe in 2014. The number of fan cafes and fan clubs has definitely increased after BTS emerged as the most popular K-pop act in Europe.

Table 5. 5 Selected K-pop Fan clubs in Europe (Source: KpopEurope December 12, 2014)

K-pop Act	Fan clubs	K-pop Act	Fan clubs
2NE1	2NE1 Hungary Fan Page Minzy (2NE1) Italy 2NE1 Romania 2NE1 Poland	2PM	It's 2PM baby ~ Italy 2PM Spain 2PM & Turkish Hottests

B1A4	B1A4 Europe B1A4 France B1A4 Germany B1A4 Italian Forum B1A4 Poland Polish BANAs B1A4 Romania	BTOB	BTOB Germany International BTOB Russia: BTOB BORN TO BEAT BTOB Turkey Offical Turkish Melody
B.A.P	European B.A.P HimChan France B.A.P B.A.P Hungary B.A.P International B.A.P Himchan B.A.P Poland B.A.P Romania B.A.P (Turkey) B.A.P_Tunisian BABY	Infinite	Infinite Germany INFINITE-FRANCE Infinite Hungary Sunggyu: Sunggyu Italia Infinite Romania INFINITE Spain INFINITE ∞ Spain UK_INFINITE
BTS	Bangtan Boys International BTS Germany Bulletproof Boy Scouts Germany Bangtan Boys Italia Bangtan Boys Romania Bangtan Boys Spanish-BTS	Beast/B2ST	BEAST Germany German B2utys for B2ST Beast Hungary Beast Turkey Turkey – Yang Yoseob B2ST Turkey B2ST International B2ST ALMIGHTY
Block B	Block B Europe Germany Block B Block B_Hungary BLOCK B Russian Fanbase	Boyfriend	Boyfriend Hungary Boyfriend Romania Spain: Boyfriend Spain
EXO	European EXOtics Exo-K France EXO D.O. – France KAI EXO France EXO XIUMIN France EXO Hungary EXO First Italian Official Fanbase EXO Italia/ Kai: Kim Jong In – Kai Italia EXO Romania EXO-K EXO-M EXOPLANET Turkey: EXO Planet [엑소] /Chanyeol: EXO Chanyeol Turkey Fan Club	Big Bang	UK BigBang FB UK BigBang Twitter Big Bang European Fan club FB/ Twitter Big Bang European Fan club Website United French VIP FB/ Twitter United French VIP Website BIGBANG Greece FB BIGBANG Greece Twitter BIGBANG V.I.P Italia FB BIGBANG V.I.P Italia Twitter/ Website Big Bang Romania FB

			Big Bang Romania Twitter Big Bang Romania Website Big Bang VK VIP BigBang RU FB VIP BigBang RU Website Big Bang Spain FB Big Bang Spain Twitter Turkey: We Are V.I.P. FB/We Are V.I.P. Twitter
LEDApple	LEDA France LED Apple Greece Italian LEDAs LED Apple Poland LEDApple Romania LEDApple_Spain LEDApple Turkey	MBLAQ	MBLA+Q% France Mblaq-France MBLAQ Italy Italy-- Vi presento gli MBLAQ Romania: MBLAQ – [Roumain Fan Page] Turkish A+ Team MBLAQ Çeviri Timi Mblaq Turkey Fan Club MBLAQ Lee Joon Fans Turkey
NU'EST	German L.O.Λ.E NU'EST Nu'est Hungary International: LOVE_for NUEST NU'EST Italia NU'EST Romania Nu'est Turkey/ Nu'est Ren Turkey	Sistar	SISTAR France Sistar Germany Sistar Hungary Sistar Romania – Oficial Sistar Spain/ STAR1 Spain
Super Junior	Super Junior Italia Siwon: Siwon Italia Shindong: Shindong Italia Russia: Super Junior VK Poland: SuJu Poland (FB) SuJu Poland (Forum) Turkey: ღTurkish ELF'sღ	TEEN TOP	TEEN TOP germany TeenTop France Teen Top French Changsters/ C.A.P France Teen Top Poland Teen Top Romania TEEN TOP VK
U-KISS	U-Kiss Me Austria U-KISS Fan (France) U-KISS Hungary KISSme Croatia U-Kiss Romania	VIXX	VIXX – German Starlights VIXX – Europe International – Leo: VIXX VIXX France VIXX Spain VIXX Turkey

***For the full list and links to fan clubs, visit the KpopEurope website (www.kpopeurope.eu).

As table 5.5 shows, the following K-pop acts have been popular in Europe since 2014. Some of the most popular groups include: B1A4, B.A.P, BTS, BEAST, and Big Bang (KpopEurope, December 12, 2014).

In addition to groups listed in table 5,5, Europe has many more fan clubs including those for F(x), F.T. Island, Fiestar, SNSD, Girl's Day, Infinite, After School, 4 Minutes, Nine Muses, Red Velvet, Seventeen, Topp Dogg, and Ze:A. Likewise, numerous unofficial K-pop fan communities exist side by side. While some clubs are individual K-pop group focused, others promote all K-pop.

CHAPTER 6

The Culture of K-pop Fandom: What do K-pop Fans do?

K-pop's global success owes to dedicated K-pop fans. They make concerted efforts to promote K-pop around the world. Fans disseminate news and information about K-pop via SNS, while creating and sharing user-generated K-pop contents via video-sharing sites. They are actively engaged in numerous collaborative fan activities worldwide. Some of the fan activities include:

Promoting K-pop via twitting and hashtag trends
Fan-driven marketing: From websites to billboards
Providing voluntary translation service
Creating K-pop reaction video
Creating Fan fiction
Covering Practices: dance, song, and play
Flash Mob Dance and Random Dance Games
Organizing K-pop cultural events
Campaigns for Social and Environmental Causes

Many observers note that the culture of K-pop fandom can be characterized as "collaborative and participatory" in nature (Jung 2011). This chapter examines the culture of K-pop fandom and fan activities in detail with some examples.

Promoting K-pop via Twitting and Hashtag

Many fans make concerted efforts to promote their favorite artists by having them nominated and ultimately chosen for prestigious music awards at various international venues. To this end, they actively participate in online-voting to nominate their favorite artists to major international music awards such as Billboard Music Awards as well as major music chart sites such as iTunes and MNET Countdown.

In addition, many K-pop fans, who live outside South Korea, have taken part in Facebook petitions or Twitter hashtag campaigns to bring their favorite group to their countries for a concert tour or to urge their broadcasting companies to play K-pop music. For instance, K-pop fans in Armenia organized a Facebook petition in 2006 to request a national TV station to broadcast Korean Pop music. Due to huge numbers of request, the Armenian TV channel *Dar 21* eventually aired K-pop music (Khachatryan (2017). Similarly, Indonesian K-pop fans organized a Facebook petition in 2011 to urge Indonesian TV stations to host K-pop acts and to request local radio stations to play K-pop music (Jung 2011). Likewise, the European ARMY, the BTS fan club in Europe, organized a hashtag movement in 2017 to get KISS FM radios all over Europe play BTS songs. To this end, they created a hashtag, #BTSonKISSFM and flooded their local radio stations with tweets asking them to play BTS songs (Koreaboo, March 9, 2017). Similar K-pop promotion campaigns took place in the Middle East. A BTS fan club in the UAE, "BTS UAE," organized a mass request project on Twitter to ask various UAE radio stations to play BTS songs. To meet the UAE fans' demand, Virgin Radio Dubai and Radio 1 UAE eventually played BTS's single "DNA" in 2017 (Khaleej Times, October 31, 2017).

Fan-driven Marketing: From Fan-run K-pop Websites to Fan-sponsored Billboards

Many fans run independent K-pop websites to disseminate information about K-pop. In Brazil, such websites include: *K-Drama, K Box, K Pop Brasil, SUJU Br, Sarangingayo, YoDramas, KPop Station*, and *Asian Mix Store.* They promote not only K-pop but also information about Korean drama and Korean culture in general. Among them, the Brazilian *Sarangingayo* website even provides an Internet radio channel for Korean music (Ko et.al. 2014). In Israel, some fans created the first online Hebrew encyclopedia on K-pop bands (Otmazgin and Lyan, 2014). Aside from online venues, some fans use off-line platforms such as magazines. Peru fan clubs have produced and distributed several Korean pop magazines including *Pop Asia, Revista I Love Korea, Mundo Asia Pop,* and *Club Kpop* in Lima (Ko et.al. 2014).

Fans utilize digital billboards to promote their favorite artists. For instance, many K-pop fans in the USA frequently use the electronic billboards in New York's Times Square to advertise their K-pop artists. The use of the Times Square billboard for one week costs about US$30,000 (Forbes, December 21, 2017). In 2017 alone, about 20-30 K-pop ad campaigns using the NASDAQ and Thomson Reuters boards took place in New York Times Square (Forbes, December 21, 2017). According to Forbes, BTS and EXO are the two most frequent K-pop groups to receive fan-sponsored billboards in Times Square (Forbes, December 21, 2017). The "BTSxSoutheast fanbase" in the USA raised over $2000 to organize an ad on the Nashville Sign to promote BTS's album "Love Yourself" in 2017 (Forbes, December 21, 2017).

Similar events take place all over the world. K-pop fans purchase ad spaces in public plazas and subway stations. In 2017, fans in Peru ran an ad to commemorate the 25th birthday of BTS member Jin

(Forbes, December 21, 2017). Baidu EXO Bar, Chinese EXO-fan community, organized an ad campaign in NY Times Square to celebrate EXO's fifth debut anniversary (Forbes, December 21, 2017). In 2018, Chinese BTS fans promoted BTS's latest songs using large LED video screens in a busy tourist spot in Las Vegas, where 38 million people visit every year (Koreaboo, May 22, 2018).

Voluntary Translation Service

Many K-pop fans voluntarily translate the lyrics of K-pop songs, news articles, interviews, TV shows and dramas that feature their favorite artists. For instance, a K-pop fan community, the ASIA4HB ("Asia for Hebrew"), in Israel has more than five thousand members who voluntarily translate Korean TV dramas and music videos (Otmazgin and Lyan, 2014). Likewise, researchers have found that some members of the ELF (Super Junior's fan club) in Peru voluntarily translate English news on K-pop to Spanish (Ko et.al. 2014). This way, information on K-pop can be widely shared among people outside Korean or English-speaking regions.

K-pop Reaction Video

YouTube and Youku are awash with user-generated K-pop videos. Among them, a K-pop reaction video is one of the most popular user-generated videos. It records people's first-time response to a K-pop music video. Typically, a reaction video entails three parts. In the first part, a video maker (a YouTuber) welcomes his or her viewers with the introduction of a music video that he or she will watch. The second part records the immediate emotional reaction of the YouTuber watching the music video which appears only in a small screen at the side. In the final part, the YouTuber discusses his or her feelings about the MV (Oh 2017; Kim 2015).

Some K-pop reaction videos attract millions of views. A K-pop reaction video, "YouTubers React to K-pop", for instance, attracted more than 22.6 million views as of August 2018.

YouTubers react to K-pop (by FBE 2013.YouTube FireShot Capture)

Due to an enormous popularity of K-pop reaction videos, some YouTubers have become celebrities themselves by attracting millions of views. Some famous K-pop reactors include: JREKML, CarKpop, ChanceMPOD, ReacttotheK, Josh Binder, TerryTV, KSpazzing, and Fomo Daily. For instance, the YouTuber JREKML has about 1.2 million subscribers and the YouTuber TerryTV has 1 million subscribers respectively as of July 2018.

K-pop Fan Fiction

Some fans write fictional stories about their favorite artists and share them online with other fans. Some fanfics are only short scripts, while others are long novels with multiple chapters. It is estimated that hundreds and thousands of K-pop fan fictions are available online sites such as Wattpad. Wattpad, one of popular writing portals for fanfiction, has over 30 million fan fiction stories. Among them, K-Pop came in fourth in "Most Popular Fanfiction Fandoms". As of 2015, EXO was named as one of the "Fastest Growing Fanfiction Fandoms" on Wattpad (Koreaboo, 18 March 2015).

Table 6.1 Examples of fanfictions (K-pop group) (Source: Lahkim 2016)

Fan Fiction Title & Author	About K-pop Artists
Miss Wanted by dbskgirl4ever	Teen Top
The Dull One by Goddess	Infinite L
The Only One by Loviet	GOT7's Jackson
A Dead Man's Diary by Exoism	EXO's Chanyeol, EXO's Baekhyun
Love Amongst Elites by dbskgirl4ever	JYJ's Jaejoong
It's a Hip- Hop World, Baby! by dbskgirl4ever	Block B's Zico
How Can It Be Him by Blackyellow	BTS's V
Two Moons by Sabooo	EXO
Red Skys and Royal Cards by Wynter	EXO

Covering practices: Dance, Song, and Play

Fans love to sing and dance to their favorite songs. The term, cover, refers to a version of a song or dance performed by fans. Fans are engaged in covering practices in all aspects of K-pop performance that include singing, dancing, and playing instruments (Jung 2011).

One can easily find many K-pop dance cover clips on YouTube. The cover dance of Groove Nation (a K-Pop dance team based in Canada) became a global sensation on YouTube after they received over five million views in just two weeks (Kim Y, 2013).

According to “United K-pop Lovers Indonesia”, there are more than 100 K-pop cover teams in Indonesia. Most cover teams have their own Facebook pages, Twitter accounts, and YouTube channels to promote their activities. Indonesian dance groups such as Massive Mix and SAYCREW produce cover dances of popular K-pop acts and make the videos available on YouTube (Muchtar 2018). One of the leading teams in Indonesia is MC Entertainment active since 2009 (Jung 2011). In Thailand, some of the top cover teams include the Wonder Gays and Ongchelic (Jung 2011). In Vietnam, the most famous K-pop cover dance groups include St.319, LYNT and YGLC, among twenty cover dance groups. Some best-known K-pop cover groups from Russia include: Boomberry, CAPSlock, Inspirit, Jayu, Luminance, MDCOV, New Nation, Party Hard, Q69, and X. EAST.

Russian cover dance "X-East" (YouTube FireShot capture)

Fans have organized cover dance contests in many countries. In 2010, over 40 teams attended a K-pop cover dance competition held in Bandung (Indonesia) (Jung 2011). The biggest cover dance contest takes place in South Korea. About 2,500 dance groups from 64 countries participated in the annual K-Pop Dance Cover Festival which was held in South Korea in 2017. The 2017 competition was watched by over 600,000 people via Twitter live. The Russian cover-dance team, "septet X.East", took the top position at the 2017 competition (Allkpop, 6 June 2017).

Aside from cover dance, fans create and share K-pop cover songs and cover plays on YouTube. Some popular YouTube channels dedicated to K-pop cover songs include: CherryLexie (YouTuber from Norway) and SeorinNorae (YouTuber from the Netherland) (Noh G, 2015). Some cover songs attract millions of views. For instance, Indonesian YouTuber, Tiffani Afifa, received over 2 million views for her K-pop cover songs (Muchtar 2018). Alongside cover songs, some fans share self-made videos showing them playing K-pop music with various instrument (Noh G, 2015).

Flash Mob Dance and Random Dance Challenge

Some fans perform flash mob dances or take part in random dance challenge games in public places. In a flash mob dance, participants dance to K-pop songs in a pre-arranged order. In contrast, in random K-pop dance games, songs are played at random and only the participants who know the choreography of the played songs can join the dancing crowd. Video clips of some random dance games such as "KPOP Random Dance Game Berlin Germany 2017" have received almost four million views as of September 2018.

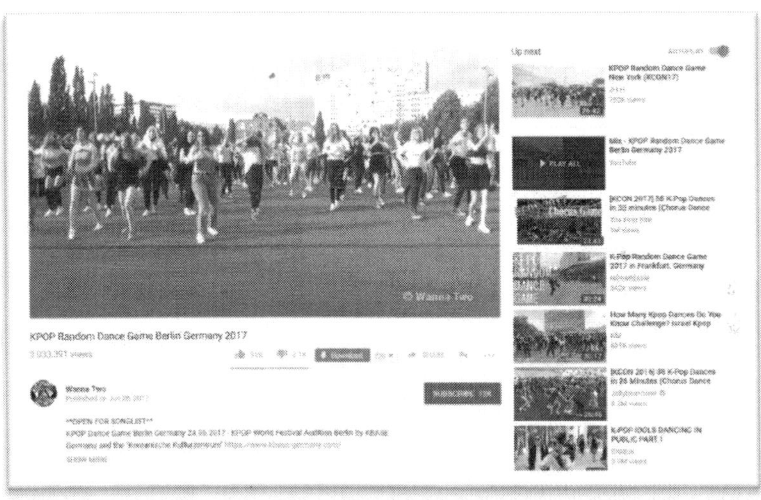

K-pop random dance challenge Berlin Germany 2017
(YouTube Fireshot)

As table 6.3 below shows, hundreds and thousands of K-pop flash mob or random dance games on YouTube are widely shared by fans around the world.

Table 6.3 K-pop Flash Mob Dance and Random Dance Challenge on YouTube

Country	Glash Mob or Random Dance Challenge
Germany	KPOP Random Dance Game Berlin Germany 2017
Italy	K-pop random dance llevado a cabo entre Miila Productions y el grupo de baile The Box en el Salón del Manga de Barcelona 2016
Israel	How Many Kpop Dances Do You Know Challenge? Israel Kpop Meeting
Brazil	Kpop Random Play Dance in Brazil - Pira Anime Fest (09/09/2018)
Vietnam	VIETNAM KPOP RANDOM DANCE IN PUBLIC 2018 || By Chuyện Fangirl (Part 1 OFFICIAL)
Lithuania	Random K-POP Dance Lithuania
Estonia	Tallinn King Sejong Institute, flash mob of K-pop dance club in front of Viru gate in Tallinn old town, in the summer of 2017.
Kazakhstan	KPOP RANDOM DANCE GAME IN PUBLIC / KAZAKHSTAN

Hosting K-pop Cultural Events

Many fan clubs are engaged in organizing K-pop related cultural events including fan gatherings and K-pop dance parties. Examples of such events in several countries are listed below.

The Philippine K-pop Committee Inc. (PKCI) organizes the Annual Philippine K-pop Convention and various other K-pop events (PKCI 2018). Together with PKCI, Cassiopeia Philippines (TVXQ's fan club in the Philippines) has helped to organize numerous K-pop events including the First Philippine K-pop Convention which took place in 2009 (PKCI 2018).

Since 2012, K-pop fans in Austria have organized local K-pop events including K-pop clubbing, K-pop karaoke, and K-pop auditions (Sung SY 2014). Anja Hillebrand, an Austrian K-pop fan, together with Bai Sujin, a voice professor at Prayner Music Conservatory in Vienna, organized the first K-pop audition show, "Austria's Next K-pop Star," in 2013 (Sung SY 2014). With the help of the Korean embassy, Christian Schleining, an Austrian K-pop fan, organized the first K-pop Dance Festival Vienna in 2013. The K-pop Dance Festival Vienna was attended by many participants from neighboring countries including Hungary, the Czech Republic, Slovakia, and France (Sung SY 2014).

In 2012, United K-pop Lovers Indonesia (UKLI) hosted Korea Sparkling Festival, inviting many K-pop artists (Jung 2011). In Israel, the largest K-pop fan group, iKpop, organized three K-pop parties in Tel Aviv in 2013 (Otmazgin and Lyan, 2014).

K-pop Fan Philanthropy: Campaigns for Social and Environmental Causes

Fan philanthropy is one of notable activities by K-pop fans around the world. In the name of their favorite K-pop artists, fans carry out social charity work or various campaigns for progressive causes.

A unique fan charity common among K-pop fans is the "wreaths of rice." For this particular fan activity, fans donate a large quantity of rice, together with wreaths of flowers bearing the name of their favorite K-pop artist, to people in poor neighborhoods. The "fan rice" has supposedly started with the fans of Shinhwa, a South Korean boy band in the 1990s. Shinhwa fans donated hundreds of kilograms of rice to a charity organization to celebrate Shinhwa's concert (Hemmeke, 2017).

Latin American fans have adopted this fan-rice tradition and called it *coronas de arroz*. For instance, several K-pop fan clubs in Peru (*Jaejoong Addiction, ELF Peru, Hato Peru, and SHINee Peru*) donated food and provided voluntary community services to people in poor areas of Lima in 2011. In Nicaragua, some fan clubs of a Korean boyband, 2PM, sent 20 kg of rice to Seoul to congratulate 2PM's performance in 2013 (Han 2017). Super Junior's fan club, E.L.F donated 110 kilograms of rice and over 1,100 packages of ramen to the Salvation Army in South Korea to commemorate Super Junior's 11th anniversary in 2017 (Hemmeke, 2017). Singaporean fans of the boy group B.A.P donated 1 ton of rice to low-income families in Singapore in 2017 (Koreaboo February 26th, 2017).

The "wreaths of rice" donated by K-pop fans (Photo credit: Shannon Yeh)

K-pop fan philanthropy extends to campaigns to protect children by raising fund for food, medical and school supplies. For instance, the

E.L.F (Super Junior's fan clubs) from more than 49 countries raised fund to build two schools, called "SJ School" in Mali, Africa. In India, EXO-L (the official fan club of EXO) donated Rs 58,000 an NGO that works for underprivileged children in Mumbai to celebrate EXO's fifth anniversary in 2017 (Gogoi 2017). The official fan club of BTS, ARMY, has been previously engaged in various charity projects that would provide medical stuff and school supplies for disadvantaged children in poor regions. In 2018, ARMY raised 1 million dollars for the UNICEF, the United Nations Children's Fund, to help children in need (Billboard, 6 May 2018).

K-pop fans are engaged in other types of charity activities, namely for an environmental cause. For instance, "Taiji Mania", the fan club of Seo Taiji and Boys in Brazil, donated about $35,000 to the World Land Trust in 2012 to protect Brazil's rainforest. The donation was earmarked to create "Seo Taiji Forest," a five-hectare section in Brazil's rainforest (Hemmeke, 2017). Similarly, Super Junior's fan club, the ELF, raised funds to plant trees in several countries including South Korea. Likewise, the fans of the girl group 2NE1 donated 1,210 mango trees and food to the village of Troj in 2012, while Shinhwa Fans have also donated 1,130 trees to Seoul City Park (Koreaboo, 26 February 2017).

Sharing the K-pop Language by Fans around the world

K-pop has left some impact on the linguistic attitude of K-pop fans who are not Koreans. As more and more non-Koreans use Korean expressions in their daily conversations or online blogging, some Korean words such as "oppa (older brother)" have entered English dictionaries.

In a case study of Algerian fans' use of Korean language, the researcher found that Algerian K-pop fans frequently use many Korean expressions in their communication with their K-pop friends

(Touhami 2017). Some of the common expressions used by Algerians are listed in table 6.4 below.

Table 6.4 Korean expressions used by K-pop fans in Algeria (Source: Touhami 2017)

Bogoshipeo: "I miss you"
Cheongmal: "really?" / "For sure"
Chingu: "friend"
Daebak: an expression to show one's surprise to someone's great luck or success.
Dang-yeonhaji: "of course"
Eonni (Unni): A woman calls her older sister or an older female friend "eonni"
Hul: Korean slang, "Oh my God"
Hwaiting: "fighting" (An expression to show one's support for others and one's own challenging endeavor)
Jebal: "please"
Komawo: "Thank you"
Kaja: "let's go"
Miahnae: "sorry"
Molla: "I do not know"
Michyeosseo: "Are you crazy?"/ "You are crazy." (Informal expression)
Nae: "yes"
Oppa: "an older brother or an older male friend" from the perspective of a girl (*Noona* is the equivalent expression for boys)
Ppalli: "quickly / fast"
Saeng-ilchugha: "happy birthday"
Saranghae: "I love you"
Yeppuda: "beautiful"

The linguistic impact of K-pop has also been noted by some journalists as well. The Indian Newspaper, "Hindustan Times", carried an article in 2017 about how Indian K-pop fans have been using the Korean language to communicate with each other. As an example, the article showed a text message on WhatsApp between two K-pop fans in India (Gogoi 2017). As the text message reads,

> "The *maknae* of the group is 13 years old. Send me the streaming link, *palli palli. Unnie*, we need to win the *daesang* this year." (*The youngest member* of the group is 13 years old. Send me the streaming link, *hurry. Sister*, we need to win *the music award* this year) (Gogoi 2017).

As the article explains, Korean language is "a secret language thousands of young people in India use in WhatsApp conversations." (Gogoi 2017). Interestingly, as table 6.4 shows, the Korean expressions used in the Indian text message are also frequently used by Algerian K-pop fans. This underscores the transnational usage of Korean language among K-pop fans.

The Power of Fans: From Passive Consumers to Active Decision-makers

Fans are not merely passive consumers of K-pop. The power of K-pop fans is so crucial for the success of K-pop artists that no label company in South Korea would do business that goes against the opinion of a significant fan base. At numerous times, fans have made concerted efforts to change label companies' decisions about the future trajectory of some K-pop acts. The recent incident involving BTS is a case in point. In 2018, Big Hit Entertainment (which manages the boyband BTS) came under fire from Korean fans for its relationship with Yasushi Akimoto, a Japanese music producer, who allegedly showed his support for Japan's colonial past. Korean fans of BTS issued a public warning that if Big Hit does not sever its relations with the controversial Japanese producer, they would boycott all products and services by Big Hit Entertainment. Eventually, Big Hit gave in to fans' pressure. The company apologized to BTS Koreans fans and cancelled its plan to release a Japanese version of BTS single, "Bird", which was made in collaboration with Yasushi Akimoto (Korea Times, 18 September 2018).

CHAPTER 7

A Brief History of K-Pop from the 1990s to the Present

This chapter provides an overview of the development of K-pop in South Korea. Before it delves into a brief history of K-pop, a definition of K-pop should be provided. Although K-pop stands for Korean pop music, it does not include all popular music originating from South Korea. In this book, K-pop is regarded as a sub-genre of Korean music which has some distinctive characteristics. As chapter 2 explained, K-pop is a highly syncretized music incorporating an extremely diverse array of musical styles, ranging from techno, EDM, rock, rap, and hip-hop to R & B, soul, reggae, house, and slow jam. In this respect, indie music, heavy metal, or traditional trot and folk songs, although still very popular among Koreans, are excluded from this chapter on the history of K-pop.

K-pop in the 1990s

When did K-pop emerge? Many K-pop observers hold the view that K-pop began in 1992 with a three-member boy band called "Seo Taiji and Boys" (Lie, 2014; Romano, 2018). Seo Taiji, the main vocalist and leader of the band, was a former-member of a heavy metal band, "Sinawe". Before the arrival of Seo Taeji and Boys, Korean music scenes were largely dominated by traditional folk songs, trot, and ballad and to a less extent by rock and heavy metal.

Seo Taeji and Boys experimented with different styles of music and incorporated not only rock elements but also rap, hip-hop, and ballad into their songs. The band was also regarded unconventional and critical in their approach to lyrical contents. Their songs dealt with controversial socio issues such as problems of Korea's competitive school system and the division of Korea. Their experimental music, together with their unconventional fashion style on stage, became very popular among young Koreans in the early 1990s. Starting with their first hit, "I Know (Nan Arayo)", the boy band paved the way for K-pop and the unique culture of K-pop fandom.

Seo Taeji in 2014 (Photo credit: Acrofan)

After Seo Taeji and Boys, more and more South Korean artists followed suit by experimenting with diverse musical styles. They further expanded the repertoire of Korean music. As table 7.1 shows, some successful K-pop acts in the 1990s include: H.O.T., Scheskies, g.o.d, Baby Vox, Shinhwa, S.E.S. and Turbo. By the late 1990s, they also became popular in China, Taiwan, and other Southeast Asian countries (Kim Y, 2013; Jolin 2017). In addition, some soloists including Park Jin-young, Kim Geon-Mo, Lee Hyori, and Lee Jung-hyun produced many hits and gained popularity in Japan and other parts of Asia. With the expanding popularity beyond South Korea, the early K-pop artists generated a unique culture of K-pop fandom which provided a cultural template for the following generations of K-pop fans.

While experimenting with various styles of music, some label companies also took innovative approaches to the process of music production including recruiting and training future performing artists. As a result, they helped to bring out numerous K-pop acts that became widely popular in the 2000s. Behind the success of earlier K-pop acts, three entertainment companies (YG, JYP, and SM) played a crucial role. The three label companies were all founded between the mid-and-late 1990s.

Table 7.1 Selected list of Popular K-pop groups and solo artists who debuted in the 1990s (Debut year)

SeoTaeji and Boys (1992), Park Jin-young (1994), Lee Hyori (1998), Lee Jung-hyun, Park Jin-young, Kim Geon-mo, Turbo (1995), Cool, Roo'ra, Hyun Jin-Young, Deux (1993), DJ Doc (1994), R.ef (1995), H.O.T (1996), Goofy (1996), Uptown (1996), Baby Vox (1997), Diva (1997), Eve (1997), NRG (1997), Sechs Kies (1997), S.E.S (1997), Fin.K.L (1998), Shinhwa (1998), Koyote (1998), Chakra (1999), As One (1999), Cleo (1999), g.o.d (1999), Fly to the Sky (1999)

K-pop in the 2000s

Some K-pop analysts note that a template or an archetype of K-pop has emerged by the end of the 2000s (Lie 2014). Although South Korea has many solo-artists and mixed-gender groups (e.g., Cool, Roora, Akdong Musician), performing as a multi-member and same -sex group became more prevalent throughout the 2000s and later remained as a norm in Korea's music industry (Lie 2014). As shown in the case with TVXQ, Big Bang, Girls' Generation, and Super Junior, most K-pop acts, debuted in the 2000s, are either boy or girl bands.

The second generation of K-pop artists in the 2000s has emulated the K-pop template that entails "attractive stars, youth-oriented lyrics, hybrid musical genres, ensemble dancing, and captivating videos" (Lie 2014). As explained in chapters 2 and 3, SNSD's "Gee" and Super Junior's "Sorry Sorry" are some typical examples of the K-pop template.

Throughout the 2000s, K-pop came to claim some significant fan bases in Asia. Some K-pop acts and soloists, with a sizable fanbase in Japan., Taiwan, Hong Kong, and China, include: BoA, Rain, Lee Hyori, 4Minute, Brown Eyed Girls, KARA and SNSD (a.k.a. Girls' Generation). Especially, KARA and SNSD ranked first and second on the *Oricon* Annual Ranking for music sales in Japan (Oricon 2010) (Jung and Hirata 2012). Oricon is the most influential popular music charts in Japan.

By the end of the 2000s, K-pop made an inroad into Europe, the Middle East, and the Americas. Several K-pop acts such as 2NE1, Wonder Girls, Super Junior, Big Bang, and SHINee became very popular in countries outside Asia.

Table 7.2 Selected list of Popular K-pop acts and soloists who debuted in the 2000s (Debut year)

BoA (2001), Ivy, Rain, Lee Hyori, Ivy, Epik High (2001), Leessang (2002), Big Mama (2003), Dynamic Duo (2003), TVXQ (2003), V.O.S (2004), SS501 (2005), LPG (2005), Super Junior (2005), Brown Eyed Girls (2006), Untouchable (2006), Big Bang (2006), Wonder Girls (2007), Kara (2007), F.T. Island (2007), Girls' Generation (2007), Supernova (2007), Davichi (2008), SHINee (2008), 2AM (2008), 2PM (2008), U-Kiss (2008), IU (2008), 2NE1 (2009), 4 Minute (2009), After School (2009), Beast (2009), f(x) (2009), MBLAQ (2009), T-ara (2009), December (2009)

K-pop Music in the 2010s

Even well before Psy's global hit, "Gangnam Style", became an international sensation in 2012, there were some signs that K-pop has emerged as a fast-growing music trend among youths in many parts of the world. An earlier sign was the SM Town Paris concert in 2011. The response of European fans to the 2011 SM Concert, which featured popular K-pop acts under SM Entertainment (e.g TVXQ, Super Junior, SNSD, and SHINee), was unprecedented in K-pop history. The two SM Town concerts in a venue for 7,000 seats were sold out in only fifteen minutes and ten minutes, respectively. In addition to online petitions signed by 4,300 European fans, some fans organized a huge protest and flash mobs at the Louvre Museum in Paris to demand additional concerts in Europe (Kang, J 2017). About 1,500 fans gathered at the airport in Paris to welcome their favorite stars. The highlights of SM Town Paris concerts uploaded on the SM YouTube channel were watched by millions of fans (Kim Y, 2013). Reflecting the growing popularity of K-Pop in Europe, the

Korean boyband Big Bang won the MTV Europe Music Awards title for "Worldwide Act" in Autumn 2011 (Kim Y, 2013).

In 2012, Psy's music video, "Gangnam Style," went viral. Psy's MV on YouTube received more than 500,000 views on the first day of its release and two month later garnered an average of nine million views per day (Tan 2015). Six months later, it became the first YouTube video with a billion views (Tan 2015). Scoring more than 3 billion as of 2018, it is marked as one of the most watched video in the *Guinness Book of World Records.* Gangnam Style won the MTV Europe Music Award for Best Video in 2012 (Tan 2015).

Before Gangnam Style emerged as a global media sensation, Psy's fame was limited only to South Korea, unlike many other K-pop acts such as Big Bang and SNSD. With his viral music video, however, Psy opened a new chapter in K-pop history. His music video has made some impacts on world politics and global pop-culture. On YouTube, millions of people all over the world created and shared "Gangnam Style" related contents including "Gangnam Style" flashmobs, cover dance, and cover songs. Many took part in such acts for amusement and pleasure, while others did so for political reasons. Psy's signature dance in Gangnam Style is the dance move pretending to swing a lasso while riding a horse. Highly profiled political figures used the "Gangnam Style" dance to gain public attention and used it as a means to get their political messages across (Rånes 2014). Such high-profile figures include: Barack Obama, the former Secretary-General of UN (Ban Ki-moon), Ai Weiwei, and some UK politicians including David Cameron.

The global success of Psy's "Gangnam Style" should not be considered as a sign that K-pop entered into the mainstream music markets of Europe and North America. The global success of "Gangnam Style" was arguably just a one-time fame for Psy due to "the funny music video, goofy dance, and a rather catchy tune" in the song (Tan 2015). As Psy's songs after Gangnam Style did not capture much attention, he gradually disappeared from the global music scenes. His viral music video, however, has generated so much media curiosity about K-pop and as a result, it provided a great opportunity to introduce other K-pop acts to the global audience.

Independently of Psy's global success, many K-pop bands continue to see their fandom grow in Asia, Europe and the Americas. Between 2013 and 2016, more than 1200 concerts were held outside of Korea. Most of these concerts were held in Japan, China and the USA. Between 2013 and 2016, over six hundred K-pop concerts were held in Japan alone (Jolin 2017). Over 2.1 million people attended K-pop concerts, hosted by SM Entertainment, between 2010 and 2012 (Jolin 2017).

From the mid 2010s onward, new K-pop acts such as EXO, BTS, and Twice became very popular in Asia, Europe, and the Americas. Especially, BTS with Big Hit entertainment has emerged as a global phenomenon with millions of fans around the world. In 2018, BTS ranked at No 1 on Billboard's World Album chart and BTS' single "Fake Love" took No. 10 on America's Billboard Hot 100. BTS concert tickets for North America (180,000 tickets) and Europe (100,000) were completely sold out within hours after they became available online in 2018 (Sim WH 2018).

Table 7.3 Selected list of Popular K-pop groups and solo artists who debuted in the 2010s

CNBLUE (2010), Girl's Day (2010), Infinite (2010), JYJ (2010), Miss A (2010), Nine Muses (2010), Orange Caramel (2010), Co-ed School (2010), Sistra (2010), Teen Top (2010), ZE:A (2010), Apink (20110, Block B (2011), Boyfriend (2011), AOA (2012), B.A.P (2012), EXID (2012), Exo (2012), NU'EST (2012), VIXX (2012), BTS (2013), Topp Dogg (2013), Akdong Musician (2014), Got 7 (2014), Mamamoo (2014), Red Velvet (2014), Winner (2014), GFriend (2015), iKon (2015), Monsta X (2015),

Seventeen (2015), Twice (2015), I.O.I (2016), Momoland (2016), Astro (2016), Cosmic Girls (2016), NCT (2016), Black Pink (2016), Pentagon (2016), K.A.R.D (2017), Pristin (2017), The Rose (2017), Dreamcatcher (2017), Wanna One (2017), Stray Kids (2018), (G)I-DLE (2018), UNB (2018), Zion. T (2011)

Korean Pop Music beyond K-pop

As for indie music, South Korea has many singer-songwriters and composers who are popular among domestic audience. For example, one of the most successful indie-rock bands in South Korea is Hyukoh. The band has produced many hits including "Wing Wing" (2014) and "Comes and goes" (2016). Aside from Korea's thriving indie music, traditional music genres such as trot, ballade and folk-songs are still very popular in the country. As mentioned in chapter 4, a trot singer, Jang Yoon-jeong, ranks as one of the top 5 most popular artist list every year. Although excluded from international attention, many Korean artists in the indie or traditional music genres produce numerous hits and have a fairly big domestic fan base.

Table 7.4 Popular Indie Musicians, Ballad and Trot Singers in South Korea

Hyukoh, BOL4, 10cm, 3rd Line Butterfly, Billy Carter,Gonne Choi, DTSQ, Patients, Adoy, Say Sue me, The Monotones, Laybricks, Dead Buttons, Yun Ddan-ddan, Standing Egg, Jang Yoon-jeong, Hong Jin-young, Cho Yong-pil, Tae Jin-ah, Im Chang-jeong, Kim Bum-soo, Park Hyo-shin, Wheesung, Hwang Chi-yeol, Yoon Sang, Kim Jong-sin, Baek Ji-young

CHAPTER 8

The Making of K-pop Stars: Label Companies, Music Producers, Choreographers and Artists

This chapter explores major players in South Korea's music industry and examines the processes through which K-pop artists come to debut. Many K-pop observers note that South Korea's music label companies have taken an innovative strategy to music production and distribution, which played a pivotal role in K-pop's global success. Equally important is the role of performing artists in the overall production of music. Do they just sing and dance to songs made by someone else? Or do they actively participate in the production of their own songs? If so, then in what capacity? This chapter will explore the complex processes of music production and distribution after providing a brief overview of major label companies in South Korea.

Korea's Innovative Music Companies

It is notable that Korea's large conglomerates, Chaebol, such as Samsung and LG, are not the major driving force behind the development of K-pop. K-pop has been developed largely by some independent label companies which started out as small music studios in the 1990s. Some of them became all-encompassing large entertainment houses by the end of 2000s. Among the most influential entertainment houses, three music studios are central players in Korea's music industry. They are: SM, YG, and JYP Entertainments. Adopting some highly innovative strategies of music production, they reportedly initiated a new era of a studio system under which future K-pop artists honed their talents and perfected their skills in all aspects of music performance (Romano, 2018; Lie 2014).

Some scholars argue that music companies' innovative and globalizing strategy may have stemmed from South Korea's highly competitive domestic music market where music companies are compelled to find new ways to outshine their competitors and to reach a new audience. Aside from business aspects, one can also reason that since good musicians have to be creative by nature and by training, they are likely to experiment with diverse musical approaches. In this regard, it should be noted that all highly successful music companies (e.g. SM, JYP, YG, and Big Hit) in South Korea were founded and are run by pop musicians themselves.

SM Entertainment

Lee Soo Man, the founder of SM, is a former singer-songwriter. He founded SM Studio, a small music company, in 1988. As his business expanded, he later changed the name to SM Entertainment in 1995. Under Lee's leadership, SM Entertainment has helped many K-pop artists to debut. As shown in table 8.1, they include: VoA, H.O.T, S.E.S., Shinhwa, SHINee, Super Junior, f(x), Girls' Generation (SNSD), TVXQ, EXO, and Red Velvet.

SM is one of the most successful entertainment houses in South Korea. Recently, Alibaba (the largest Chinese e-commerce conglomerate) has invested $30 million into SM Entertainment to tap into the growing K-pop market in Asia and beyond (Yoon 2017).

YG Entertainment

Yang Hyun-suk, a former member of Seo Taiji and Boys, founded YG Entertainment in 1998. Under his leadership, YG has trained many K-pop bands and soloists. Some famous K-pop groups with YG include: 2NE1, Big Bang, Winner, iKon, and Black Pink. As for YG's famous soloists, they include: Psy, Wheesung, B.I., Bobby, Gummy, Zion. T, and Teddy Park. YG's founder, Yang Hyun-suk, has regularly appeared in many TV music competition shows such as "Mix Nine" and "K-pop Stars".

JYP Entertainment

Park Jin-young, a singer-song writer and dancer, founded JYP Entertainment in 1997. Even today, Park still maintains his music career as a performing artist and composer, while managing JYP Entertainment.

Under Park's leadership, JYP Entertainment has helped many K-pop artists to produce numerous hits. Some very successful artists under JYP include: Wonder Girls, GOT7, 2PM, 2AM, Miss A and TWICE. Seven songs from GOT7 made it to the top 15 of *Billboard*'s World Albums charts. TWICE, a multinational nine-member act, became the best-selling K-pop girl group in 2017 (Herman 2018).

JYP is expanding its operation beyond South Korea. Starting from 2017, JYP partnered with China's Tencent Music Entertainment Group to have their first Chinese boyband "Boy Story" to debut in China (Herman 2018). Park Jin-young has produced all five pre-debt singles that the six-member boyband, Boy Story, released in China.

The international success of K-pop is reflected in the growing overseas revenue of the major entertainment houses. South Korea's music industry as a whole is valued at $ 5billion (Romano, 2018). Between 2007 and 2012, SM Entertainment's overseas revenue increased more than 20-fold. YG Entertainment saw a similar growth, where the overseas revenue has doubled between 2011 and 2012 (Shin and Kim, 2013).

Table 8.1 Top 3 Music Agencies and their K-pop Acts

Agency	K-pop Groups and Solo Artists (Debut Year)
JYP	Wonder Girls, Twice, 4 Minute, Rain, GOT7, 2PM, 2AM, Miss A, G. Soul, DAY 6, g.o.d., J J Project, Stray Kids', Twice
SM	H.O.T (1996), SHINee, BoA (2001), Super Junior, Girls' Generation (SNSD), F(x), TVXQ (2003), Shinhwa (1998), S.E.S (1997), Fly to the sky (1999), EXO, Red Velvet, NCT
YG	Epik High, iKon, Winnter, Sechs Kies, Jinusean, Akdong Musician, Psy, Black Pink, Gummy, Zion.T, 2NE1, Big Bang, and SE7EN, CL, WINNER, 1TYM, DJ Tukutz, Kang Seung-Yoon, Minzy, Dara, Sandara Park, Stony Skunk, Katie Kim, Lee Hi, Tablo, Taebin, Teddy Park, iKon, MOBB, Wheesung, Big Mama

Although the influence of the three label companies over Korea's music industry has been dominant, numerous other music companies are striving to gain influence and more market shares (Shin and Kim, 2013).

Other Label Companies

Beyond the big three, other label companies have helped many K-pop acts to rise to global stardom. Big Hit is a case in point. The global K-pop boyband, BTS, is not with one of the three major agencies but with the previously unknown small label company, Big Hit. The company was founded by a former JYP songwriter "Hitman" (his real name is Bang Si Hyuk) in 2005. With the success of BTS, Big Hit has become one of the most valued music companies in South Korea. Big Hit's market value alone is today estimated at $1.85billion (Guardian, 5 June 2018).

Table 8.2 Other Label Companies with Popular K-pop Acts

Entertainment House	Artists
FNC Entertainment	CNBLUE, FT Island, N. Flying, AOA, AOA Cream, Hong-gi, Yonghwa, Jimin, Choa, Jong-hyun, InnoVator, SF9, and Juniel
CUBE Entertainment	PENTAGON, BTOB, CLC, Yook Sungjae, Yoon Doojoon, HyunA, Ga Yoon, G. NA, Jang Hyun Seung, and Lee Gikwang.
Starship Entertainment	Cosmic Girls, Monsta X, Yoo Seung Woo, Hyorin, Soyou, K. Will, Mad Clown, Brother Su, Boyfriend, WJSN, JungGiGo, and SISTAR
Big Hit Entertainment	BTS and Homme
Pledis Entertainment	NU'EST, SEVENTEEN, Orange Caramel, UEE, Han Don Geun, Pledis Girlz, Pristin, After School.
Wollim Entertainment	Infinite, Lovelyz, JOO, Nell
Star Empire Entertainment	9 MUSES and IMFACT

As for the role of Korea's big conglomerates (chaebol) in South Korea's music industry, it is largely limited to the distribution and marketing aspect of music. Except CJ E&M, a subsidiary of the CJ Group, they do not play a significant role in the production of music and training pop artists.

Table 8.3 Smaller label companies in South Korea

Maroo Entertainment, Brand New Music, MMO, LOEN Entertainment, TS Entertainment, Jellyfish Entertainment, YMC Entertainment, WM Entertainment, Plan A Entertainment, Stone Music Entertainment, J Tune Entertainment, Fantagio, Brave Entertainment, B2M Entertainment, Starship Entertainment, AB Entertainment, 100% Entertainment, Illusion Entertainment and All-S Entertainment

The Making of K-pop Stars: The System of Music Production, Artist Training, and Marketing

Korea's music industry is highly competitive since many K-pop acts and a countless number of K-pop star hopefuls strive to gain attention. About 300-400 K-pop acts are reportedly active in South Korea but a majority of K-pop artists have a very slim chance (only 0.001% according to some media) to rise to national or global stardom (Channel A, 4 May 2018).

Against this backdrop of cut-throat competition, K-pop artists are expected to show a high degree of professionalism in all aspects of music performance including song-writing, singing, dancing, public speaking, and managing their public persona. To this end, most music agencies, albeit to a varying degree, have adopted a systematic and highly innovative approach to the production of music and the training of artists. Their star-producing system entail some of the following approaches, albeit smaller label companies may not have economic resources to employ all the measures described below.

Music Production

From song writing to album production, major Korean music companies have taken an innovative approach which stresses experimental music through very collaborative work processes drawing on domestic and foreign talents.

South Korea has many talented singers, composers, songwriters, and choreographers. For song-writing and creating soundtrack, all label companies tap into a large pool of Korea's prolific songwriters and composers. As table 8.4 shows, some of South Korea's best-known composers and song writers include: Shin Hyuk (Joombas Music Group), Shinsadong Tiger, Slow Rabbit, Pdogg, Brave Brothers, E-Tribe, Sweetune, Teddy Park, and Black Eyed Pilseung, among many others (Beyond Hallyu 2012).

Sin Hyuk, a singer-songwriter and music producer, has earned his fame by co-producing and co-writing Justin Bieber's "One Less Lonely Girl" (2009). Afterwards, he founded his own music producing company, Joombas Music Group, and has worked with numerous K-pop artists including EXO, SHinee, f(X), SNSD, and Teen Top.

Brave Brothers (his real name: Kang Don-chul) is a former composer and producer for YG Entertainment. Under YG, he helped to produce two of Big Bang's first big hits, "Lies" and "Last Farewell" (Byond Hallyu 2012). After leaving YG in 2008, he established his own label company, Brave Entertainment. As table 8.4 shows, he has co-produced and co-written many K-pop hits for After School, Sistar, U-Kiss, and Big Bang among many others.

YG has its own composers and songwriters within the company including Teddy Park, iKon's B.I., Big Bang's G-Dragon and T.O.P, Choice37, Lydia Paek and Kush (Koreaboo, 13 December 2017). Among them, Teddy Park has co-produced many hits including Big

Bang's "Fantastic Baby", Black Pink's "Whistle" and Psy's "Daddy".

Black Eyed Pilseung, a song-writing and record producing duo, has worked with many K-pop artists especially JYP's acts including TWICE (Yoon 2017). The duo produced many Twice' hits including Twice's "TT" and "Cheer up". In 2016, Black Eyed Pilseung won the Best Producer of the Year Award at Mnet Asian Music Awards.

Shinsadong Tiger (his real name: Lee Ho-yang) is one of the most prolific songwriters and record producers in South Korea. As he previously worked for Cube Entertainment, he produced numerous hits for T-ara, 4Minute and Beast (Beyond Hallyu 2012). Later, Shinsadong Tiger founded his own label, AB Entertainment and the Modern K Music Academy. One of famous K-pop acts with AB Entertainment is a girl group, EXID.

Pdogg works with Big Hit Entertainment. He is one of the main co-producers behind many of BTS' hits including "Fire," "Dope," and "Spring Day, and "DNA". In 2017, Pdogg has won the Best Producer Award at the Mnet Asian Music Awards. Together with Pdogg, Slow Rabbit (his real name: Kwon Do Hyeong) has also contributed to BTS albums including "The Most Beautiful Moment in Life", "You never walk alone", and "Love Yourself".

Many other producers and songwriters have contributed to K-pop hits. They include: Double Sidekick, Lee Min-soo, Yoo Young-Jin, E-Tribe, among many others. Double Sidekick has produced hits for Baek Ji-young and T-ara, Lee Minsoo is responsible for most of the releases of LOEN Entertainment and Nega Network artists. Lee Minsoo is behind most of IU, Brown Eyed Girls and Sunny Hill's biggest hits (Beyond Hallyu 2012). Sweetune (Han Jae-ho and Kim Seung-soo) has created many of KARA's biggest hits including "Mister". They have also written a string of hits for Infinite and many of Boyfriend and Nine Muses' singles (Beyond Hallyu 2012). Yoo Young-jin co-produced many soundtracks for SM acts (Koreaboo, 13 December 2017). Kim Dohoon has co-written many hits for K.Will, Soyou and Junggigo. He also composed CNBLUE's hit, "I'm A Loner" (Beyond Hallyu 2012). E-Tribe, a record production duo, composed many hits including Girls' Generation's "Gee" and Miss A's "Hush". The founder of JYP, Park Jin-young, himself has composed and co-written many hits for his own albums as well as for JYP artists.

In addition, as chapter 11 discusses in detail, individual members of K-pop groups such as Big Bang, BST, Pentagon, Block B, iKON and SHINee have actively taken part in composing and writing lyrics of their own songs. For instance, B.I., a member of iKON, has co-produced many hits for the group and others including Winner, Psy, and Black Pink (Koreaboo, 13 December 2017). Likewise, Suga and RM from BTS have co-written and co-produced many of BTS hits including "Blood, Sweat & Tears" (Koreaboo, 13 December 2017). Zico from Block B has been a prolific songwriter, as more than 93 works are credited to him (Koreaboo, 13 December 2017).

Table 8.4 Korean K-pop Composers and Songwriters

Record Producer/Composers & Songwriters	Examples of co-produced/ co-written works
Shinsadong Tiger (Real Name: Lee Ho-yang)	4 Minute's "Hot Issue", "Mirror Mirror" BEAST's "Soom", "Shok", "Fiction", "Mystery" A Pink's "No No No" & "Five" Ailee's "U& I" Momoland's "Bboom Bboom" EXID's "DDD", "Lady", "L.I.E.", "Up & Down" Hyun A's "Bubble Pop!" VIXX's "Rock Ur Body", "Only U" T-ara's "One & One"

Sin Hyuk (Joombas Muisic Group)	Justin Bieber's "One Less Lonely Girl" (2009) EXO's "Engel", "Growl", "Dpn't go", "Black Pearl" Shinee's "Dream Girl" VIXX's "Light Me Up" and "G.R.8.U" f(x)'s "Pretty Girl" & " 100%'s "Want U back" Girls' Generation's "Romantic St." TVXQ's "Heaven's Day" Teen Top's "Supa Luv"
Teddy Park	Big Bang's "FXXK IT", "Fantastic Baby" BLACKPINK's "Whistle" Taeyang's " Only Look At Me", "Eyes, Nose, Lips" Psy's "Daddy" iKon's "Apology" Sunmi's "Gashina" 2NE1's "I don't care" CL's "The Baddest Female"
Brave Brothers (Real Name: Kang Dong-chul)	U-Kiss' "Manmanhani" "Round & Round", "Without you." Big Bang' s "Wonderful", "Oh my baby" 4 Minute's "What is my name?" "Is it poppin'?" After School's "Diva", Play Girlz", "AH" Sistar's "Here we come", "Push push", "How dare you", "Come closer" Teen Top's "Be Ma Girl", "Don't I", "Except for me", "Love is"
Slow Rabbit (Real Name: Kwon Do Hyeong)	BTS Albums (The Most Beautiful Moment in Life, You never walk alone, Love Yourself)
B.I.	iKon's "Welcome Back", "Rhythm Ta", "My Type", "Today", "Airplane", "Anthem", "Bling Bling", "B-Day", "Beautiful", "Long Time No See" Epik High's "Born Hater" Winner's "Empty" Black Pink's "Whistle"
Black Eyed Pilseung (Song Joo-young and Choi Kyu-sun)	Sistar's "Touch my body" Miss A's "Only You" Twice's "Like Ooj Ahh", "Likey", "TT", and "Cheer up"

Pdogg (Gang Hyowon)	BTS' "Fire", "I need you", "Dope," "Spring Day", "DNA"
E-Tribe (Ahn Myung-won and Kim Young-deuk)	Girls' Generation's "Gee" Miss A's "Hush" Lee Hyo-ri's "U-Go-Girl" T-ara' "Yayaya" Super Junior's "It's You"
Ryan S Jhun	Taeyeon's "Something New" EXO's "Cloud 9" I.O.I's "Watta Man" Red Velvet's "Camp Fire", "Red Dress"

As Pdogg, the co-producer of numerous BTS' hits, pointed out, music production is a highly collaborative process in which a song is built up on numerous sound bites and phrases drawn from multiple producers. In an interview, Pdogg describes the "very collaborative process" through which BTS songs came into existence. As he explains it,

> "It varies for each song, but we typically create a general framework based on the members' outlook on modern-day society or their current emotional state. Then, using that as a basis, we begin more concrete production. There are also some instances when I set the song up first, and the members complete it by adding their contributions. Each song is different, so we don't have a fixed system. If you compare it to a puzzle, I guess you could say that the members each create individual pieces, and I play the role of choosing the best pieces to put together a completed image." (Cha 2017)

The collaborative nature of music production is underscored by how many individuals with different nationalities have been involved in the production of one music album. "For example, the credits for the highly successful girl group Girls' Generation's album *I Got a Boy* list 74 individuals: 36 are credited as songwriters, and 15 are credited as producers. These contributors are from Korea, USA, the Netherlands, Ireland, Wales, England, Denmark, Morocco, Sweden, and Norway" (Rånes 2014).

Aside from domestic talents, as table 8.5 shows, label companies also use foreign composers and songwriters to create K-pop hits. The foreign producers, who worked with many K-pop artists, include: Dsign Music (Norway), DeepFrost (Norway), LDN Noise (Britain), Caesar & Loui and Andreas Öberg (Sweden) and Kevin Randolph, Davey Nate, and Devine-Channel (the USA).

Dsign Music, a Norway based composition and production company, has closely worked with SM Entertainment (Kim SY 2016). It has contributed to the 27 K-pop tracks including some of famous tracks such as SNSD's "I Got a Boy," and "Tell Me Your Wish (Genie)" (Rånes 2014). Norwegian producers of DeepFrost together with the American songwriter Ursula Yancy have worked for JYP Entertainment by producing some tracks for K-pop groups such as Miss A (Rånes 2014).

Table 8.5 Collaboration with foreign composers (source: Oh and Park 2012)

Entertainment Houses	Foreign composers working with /K-pop artists
SM	Busbee, Alex James, Kalle Engstrom, Harvey Mason Jr/ Girls Generation Oslo Recording/ Super Junior Jeff Hoeppner, Thomas Troelsen, Willem Laseroms/ f(x) NaoKanata, RyojiSonoda/BoA and TVXQ Thomas Troelsen/ SHINee
YG	Daishi Dance/ Big Bang Nagao Dai/ SE7EN
JYP	Claude Kelly/ Wonder Girls

SM Entertainment reportedly collects 400–500 demo songs from foreign composers per year. It even organized a song-writing camp (called "Fantasia") in 2013, in which some twenty composers and song-writers from Sweden, Denmark, Norway, England, and Germany were given detailed instructions to create some twenty demo soundtracks for SM artists (Kim SY 2016; Jolin 2017).

Aside from composing and song-writing, music production entails also choreographing. As table 8.6 shows, many professional choreographers in South Korea have contributed to some of the most famous signature dance moves associated with K-pop hits. Some of the best-known Korean choreographers include: Kim Tae-Woo, Honey J, Bae Yoon -Jung, Mina Myoung, Jay Kim, Lia Kim, May J Lee, Hyojin Choi and Sori Na.

Bae Yoon-Jung has choreographed many K-pop songs including Brown Eyed Girls' "Abracadabra", Kara's "Mister", EXID's "Up and Down", and T-ara's "Bo Beep Bo Beep" (Lee L 2017). Honey J (real name: Hanee Jeong) is the leader of all-female hip-hop dance crew Purplow. She has made choreographies for Jay Park, Hyorin, Hyoyeon, and Sistar (Lee L 2017).

Table 8.6 Korean choreographers (Source: Heytoto 2016/ Lee L 2017)

Choreographer (Affiliation)	Working with K-pop acts (Choreographed work)
Blazer Pyo (JYP)	JYP Artists Miss A's Suzy
Kim Tae-Woo (aka Kasper)--(1 Million Dance School)	SM Entertainment artists Taemin (Drip Drop)/ EXO (Ko Ko Bop)

Choi Jun Ho (1 Million Dance School)	INFINITE
Ko Kyung-jun (DQ Agency)	ASTRO/SISTAR and MONSTA X
Mina Myoung (1 Million Dance School)	Jessi (Gucci)
Lia Kim (1 Million Dance School)	I.O.I (Very Very Very), TWICE (TT, Like Ooh Ahh), Sunmi (Full Moon, 24 Hours) and BoA (Fox).
Sori Na (1 Million Dance School)	Rihanna (Work).
Bae Yoon-Jung	Brown Eyed Girls (Abracadabra)/ Kara (Mister, Mamma Mia)/ EXID (Up and Down, Ah Yeah)/ T-ara (Bo Beep Bo Beep, Lovey Dovey)/ Girls Day (Expectation, Something)
Honey J (Purplow)	Jay Park (You Know, Thinking About You, Me Like Yuh)/ Sistar (Bora)

Several South Korean dance schools including the DQ Agency Dance Team, and 1 Million Dance School have some amazing choreographers (Heytoto 2016). Several choreographers from 1Million Dance Studio have closely worked with many K-pop artists including Girls' Generation and 2NE1. Lia Kim (a choreographer of the 1 Million Dance School), for instance, helped to choreograph TWICE's "TT" and "Like Ooh Ahh", Sunmi's "Full Moon", and BoA's "Fox" (Lee L 2017). Ko Kyung-jun from the DQ Agency has helped with choreography for a boy group ASTRO (Heytoto 2016).

Table 8.7 Examples of K-pop artists with choreography skills (Source: SBS Pop Asia 2018)

Individual Name (Group)	Choreographed Dance
Shindong (Super Junior)	Many Super Junior's hits

Hoshi (Seventeen)	Seventeen's "Adore U"
Chung Ha	I.O.I's "Whatta Man"
Taehyun (Hotshot/ JbJ)	Jelly
N (VIXX)	MYTEEN's "Take It Out" VIXX tracks
Kino (Pentagon)	"Like This" and "Runaway"
Jihun (KNK)	KNK songs/ HALO's "O.M.G"
Rocky (Astro)	"Fireworks"

In addition to professional choreographers, as table 8.7 shows, many K-pop stars themselves have contributed to the creation of choreographies of their own songs. Super Junior's Shindong, for instance, is the main choreographer for the group.

Some larger entertainment houses have taped into the global pool of world-class choreographers. As table 8.8 shows, some world renowned foreign choreographers have helped to produce the choreography of many K-pop hits. They include: Parris Goebel, Tony Testa, Keone Madrid, and Ian Eastwood (Lee L 2017).

Table 8.8 Foreign choreographers (Source: Lee L 2017)

Choreographer	K-pop artists (Choreography)
Keone Madrid	BTS (Fire, Dope), 2PMm (A.D.T.O.Y), Got7 (Just Right), VIXX, B1A4, Monsta X and Taeyang
Sugawara Koharu	2NE1 (Falling in Love), Taemin (Sayonara Hitori) and SNSD (Love & Girls).
Kyle Hanagami	BlackPink (Boombayah), f(x) (4 Walls), Red Velvet (Ice Cream Cake), BlackPink
Parris Goebel	Big Bang (Bang Bang Bang/ Ringa Linga/ Good Boy), ikon (Rhythm Ta), 2NE1, Crush, 4Minute (Crazy).
Tony Testa	TVXQ (Catch Me/ Something), SNSD (Lion Heart), EXO (Wolf / Overdose). SHINee (Married to Music/

	Everybody/ Sherlock/ Dream Girl), Super Junior (*Devil / Mamacita*)
Rino Nakasone	SHINee (Replay/ Juliette/ Lucifer), SNSD (Genie/ Oh!/ The Boys), TVXQ (Keep Your Head Down/ Maximum), f(x) (Chu/ Nu Abo/ Hot Summer) and Red Velvet (Rookie)
Ian Eastwood	Taemin (Danger), SHINee (View)

Parris Goebel from New Zealand has worked with some famous American artists including Justin Bieber, J. Lo, Rihanna and Nicki Minaj. She choreographed Justin Bieber's music video for “Sorry,” which attracted over 2.2 billion views (Lee L 2017). As for K-pop, she has helped to choreograph Big Bang’s “Bang Bang Bang”, “Ringa Linga”, and “Good Boy” (Lee L 2017).

Tony Testa has worked with global super-stars such as Britney Spears, Jennifer Lopez, and Michael Jackson. As for K-pop, Tony has worked with SM artists and helped to choreograph EXO’s “Wolf” and “Overdose”, Super Junior’s “Devil” and “Mamacita”, and TVXQ’s “Something” and “Catch me” (Rowe 2016). Keone Madrid, who has worked with Justin Bieber, choreographed many K-pop hits. They include: BTS’ “Fire” and “Dope” and Got7’s “Just Right”, among many others (Rowe 2016).

Music production is a highly complex and collaborative process that also involves visual presentation of music, i.e., making music videos. Behind K-pop’s global success, there are hidden talents who produce some amazing music videos that capture K-pop’s impressive choreography in colorful, dynamic, and eye-pleasing music videos.

In South Korea, only a handful of MV production companies are responsible for K-pop MVs. Having produced most K-pop MVs, Zanybros and Digipedi are the two largest companies. Established in 2001, Zanybros has worked with almost all K-pop stars. The company has produced more than 1,000 MVs, including SNSD's "Boys", B.A.P.'s "One Shot". Some smaller companies (Lumpens, VM Project, and GDW) are catching up with the two biggest companies, as they have recently taken up a more active role in producing MV hits. For instance, GDW has produced MVs for BTS' "Dope," "Save Me," and "Not Today."

It should be noted that MV production is quite pricy, as the production cost ranges somewhere between US$200,000 and over one million dollars (Guardian, 5 June 2018). The MV of Big Bang's "Love Song" costed US $200,000, while close to one million dollars were spent for the production of MVs for B.A.P.'s "One shot" and T-ara's "Cry Cry" (Koreaboo, 11 May 2018). The high cost of music video is one of the reasons why most K-pop star hopefuls seek an organizational sponsorship from well-established label companies. Only those larger companies with substantial financial resources can produce high quality MVs for their artists.

Table 8. 9 Korean MV Production Companies

MV Production Company	K-pop acts (MV title)
Zanybros	Hundreds of major K-pop MVs including SNSD (Boys), B.A.P. (One Shot), Super Junior (Devil), Wanna One (Energetic).
Digipedi	Psy (Daddy), Infinite (Bad), EXID (DDD), Seventeen (Call, call, call)
Lumpens	VIXX (Love Equation) / BTS (Wings)
VM Project	Exo (Monster, Love me right, Light saber), Blackpink (Whistle), Red velvet (Dumb Dumb)
GDW	BTS (Dope/ Save Me/ Not Today/Mic Drop)/ Red Velvet (Happiness/ 'Ice Cream Cake), Taemin (Danger)

Naive Creative	Most JYP MVs & GOT7 MVs

In essence, K-pop music is the product of highly collaborative team work involving many experts and talents in many areas. Professionals all over the world contribute to the varied aspects of music production ranging from creating a soundbite to choreography and MV directing.

Artist Recruitment

Many K-pop star hopefuls, most in their early teens, are recruited through highly competitive auditions. Most K-pop label companies regularly audition people. Some larger companies such as JYP, YG and SM entertainments provide auditions weekly, monthly as well as annually. Some companies hold auditions around the world to search for global talents. For instance, SM Entertainment held its global audition in 50 cities across 10 countries, including China, the US, Japan, Canada, Thailand, Chile, Argentina, and Vietnam in 2018 (Hong DY, 2018).

It is estimated that SM Entertainment selects about 1 trainee for every 1,000 applicants, while other agencies claim roughly 1 acceptance for every 250 applicants (Sin 2018). In addition to the annual studio auditions, there are other venues through which potential K-pop stars get scouted by music agencies. They include online and public TV audition. V-Square is a K-pop online audition platform open to all candidates around the world. Due to a low application fee (US $2.99), the online platform provides a great opportunity for the talented singer to be exposed to music agencies. It also provides music companies a chance to do primary screening and evaluations of international applicants. Sand Factory, a renowned vocal training facility in South Korea, examines applicants for the primary evaluations. Most smaller label companies such as 100% Entertainment, Illusion Entertainment and All-S Entertainment utilize V-Square to recruit global talents.

In addition, some talented singers are also scouted through TV music competition shows similar to "American Idol" and "X-Factor". Some best-known TV audition shows in South Korea include: *K-pop Star, Show Me the Money, Super Star K, and High School Rapper*, among many others.

Against this backdrop of high competition among the K-pop star hopefuls, many private K-pop academies and special music schools have sprung up in South Korea. Private music academies are designed to prepare youngsters for K-pop auditions by providing extensive singing and dance lessons after school. For instance, "Def Dance Skool", one of such K-pop academies, had about one thousand students as of 2013 (Jolin 2017). Another private academy, "Move", had more than 500 students as of 2016 (Power, 2016). In contrast to private academies (*hakwon*), some private music schools are full-fledged high schools with comprehensive educational curricula. Seoul Music High School (SMHS), for instance, offers government-approved regular high school courses with a focus on K-pop music. The SMHS has taught many students who later became successful K-pop stars. Some high-profile students include: Jong-Hyun (SHINee), Jung-Min (Boyfriend), VA-ra (Hello Venus), and Zico (Block-B). It currently has more than 7,000 students enrolled (Kpop College 2018).

Artist Training

Once teenagers get scouted by label companies, they become trainees who undergo a period of musicianship training before they debut. During the training process, label companies provide special educational programs to their trainees. The educational curricula include various lessons including singing, dancing, music composition and learning foreign languages (English, Mandarin, and Japanese). Trainees also receive lessons how to behave as a public person and a respectable pop star. For SM Entertainment, about seventy instructors taught SM trainees in 2013 (Kim Y, 2013). JYP's training center offers sixty-seven different subjects. With the help of the systemized traineeship, many K-pop trainees learn to become multilingual and multi-skilled entertainers. For instance, BoA learned both Japanese and English under SM's training system (Jung and Hirata 2012). It should be noted that the systematized traineeship requires a substantial investment from music agencies. For instance, SM invested about $3 million in BoA's debut. As for the training program in 2013 alone, SM Entertainment supposedly spent more than US $5 million (Shin and Kim, 2013).

Observers of Korean music industry note that the training period can last from three to eight years. For instance, four of the nine member-girl group, SNSD, were trained for six years. Since K-pop training processes are known to be very arduous, almost resembling a boot-camp, some critics deride the musicianship training as a 'factory-like system of grooming and training stars' (Sin, 2018) or "a training institute for Olympic athletes" (Lie 2014). People should, however, put the K-pop training system in the South Korean context. In South Korea's highly competitive educational environment, K-pop training is no more or no less competitive and grueling than a regular schooling that millions of students undergo to prepare for a university entrance exam.

Not all trainees can make it to an official debut. It is reported that on average, only one in ten trainees is likely to be casted in a K-pop act (Jolin 2017). A popular South Korean TV talent show *Produce 101* underscores how hard it is for trainees to become a K-pop star. The show has recently drawn tremendous attentions in Korea and abroad. In the *Produce 101* show, in which hundred and one trainees from various label companies compete against each other, only 11 contestants get selected. The chosen candidates get a chance to debut as a new K-pop act only just for one year. Wanna One, a highly popular new K-pop act, is such a case. In 2017, the 11-member boyband came into being through *Produce 101*. With their debut single, "Energetic", Wanna One quickly rose to national stardom (Romano, 2018).

Wanna One, the 11 winners of the Produce 101, K-pop star trainees competition show (Photo © DaftTaengk)

Music Performance: From Soloists to Group Members

After a long period of arduous traineeship, successful trainees get placed into a boy or girl band and only a selected few get to perform as a solo artist. In fact, some observers note that the way most music label companies groom their trainees is largely group oriented rather than preparing them as solo artists. Debuting as a group, however, does not exclude individual members from performing as soloists. It is quite common that most members, if not all, of major K-pop bands maintain their career as soloists while they take part in group activities.

Some observers note that music agencies have multiple reasons for favoring a group formation. It is argued that the group structure maximizes chances for media exposure. For instance, some members may appear in TV dramas and variety shows, while others are engaged in promotional activities such as fan meetings or music production. The longevity as a group is better secured, even when a member cannot continue as a performer for various reasons (Lie 2014).

Nowadays, K-pop bands tend to be multinational in the sense that many have at least one non-Korean member. Multinational group formation, another innovation on the part of K-pop music agencies, greatly expands chances to appeal to a bigger audience. To expand the linguistic ability of the group, music agencies recruit artists of non-Korean nationalities or members of the Korean diaspora who are bilingual. For instance, F(x) is a five-member group consisting of girls from China, Korea, Taiwan and the US. JYP Entertainment's girl group, Miss A, also includes two Chinese members, Fei and Jia. The group 2PM includes Nickkhun, an American of Thai-Chinese descent, who speaks at least three languages fluently. SNSD's Two members are Korean-Americans, while another speaks fluent Japanese. EXO has members capable of performing in Mandarin and Japanese. EXO-M (Chinese) operated in sinophone countries (China, Hong Kong, Taiwan, and Singapore), while EXO-K concentrated on South Korean audience. JYP's girl group, Twice, has 3 Japanese, 1 Taiwanese, and 5 Korean members. Black Pink has 2 Korean, 1 Thai and 1 Australian members. Like EXO, Super Junior also performed as Super Junior-M (Chinese singers) and Super Junior-K (Korean singers).

In addition, many K-pop artists produce albums in multiple languages such as Chinese and Japanese. Given that Japan is the second largest music market in the world, many K-pop groups made Japanese versions of their hits. Major K-pop acts such as TVXQ, Super Junior, Big Bang and BTS have produced their albums both in Korean and Japanese. VoA produced her albums in four languages (Korean, Chinese, Japanese and English). Baby V.O.X., which gained popularity across Asia in the late 1990s and early 2000s, released their album, in four languages (English, Chinese, Japanese, and Korean). Wonder Girls also released their hit, "Nobody", in four different languages. Rain's third album, 'It's Raining', has a special track with a Thai version of the song 'I Do', since he was very popular in Thailand.

Although music agencies produce multi-lingual albums, it is either by having Korean singers sing in Japanese or Mandarin or by having Chinese or Japanese members sing in their native language. English version of K-pop is, however, still limited. Some K-pop artists including Wonder Girls, CL, and Super Junior's Henry have produced English singles. For most K-pop artists, they use only catchy English phrases to reduce language barriers.

Music Distribution and Marketing

In the early days of K-pop development, music companies heavily relied on producing multi-lingual albums to target foreign markets. In the era of Web 2.0, localization strategy (promoting music in the language of the consumer country) has been losing its importance. Nowadays, they focus less on multi-lingual albums but rather more on digital media technology, particularly social media, to attract non-Korean listeners. Since online streaming, social networking sites and video sharing portals have become the major channels for the distribution of K-pop, IT technology has greatly accelerated the transcultural border crossing of K-pop to reach non-Korean audience.

Digital marketing is crucial for K-pop's success. Entertainment companies actively utilize multiple social media platforms (Twitter, Facebook, Weibo, etc.) for K-pop marketing. With music videos ever more important, most label companies have their own YouTube and Youku channels to attract millions of viewers around the world. As of September 2018, Bangtan TV, BTS official YouTube channel, has 11 million subscribers, while its Chinese Youku channel has about 4.89 million views.

To expand the distribution of K-pop and media exposure, some larger Korean label companies set up subsidiaries in foreign countries or enter into a partnership agreement with foreign counterparts and record distributors. For instance, YG Entertainment established its subsidiaries such as YGEX in Japan, YG USA and YG Hong Kong in 2012 (Shin and Kim, 2013). Additionally, some label companies extended their business in other areas of entertainment industry. For instance, SM Entertainment has set up SM Pictures, a film producer subsidiary in 2007, and has produced many films that featured SM artists (Shin and Kim, 2013).

It is notable that major music agencies such as SM, YG, and JYP are not just music agencies but function as multi-faceted entertainment houses. In other words, they work with TV broadcasting companies and the film industry to get their stars appear on TV variety shows, dramas, and movies. As mentioned in previous chapters, many K-pop artists have a career as actor and/or TV personality.

CHAPTER 9

K-pop in the Context of the Korean Wave (Hallyu)

The growing popularity of K-Pop should be understood in the context of the Hallyu (the Korean Wave) movement that emerged in the late 1990s. The term, Hallyu (the Korean Wave), which was coined by Chinese media in the mid-1990s, initially refers to the popularity of Korean TV dramas in Asia. The term later developed into a broad cultural category denoting the popularity of all Korean cultural contents including K-pop, fashion, cuisine, and cosmetics.

Some scholars identify two distinctive phases of the Korean Wave, i.e., the First Wave and the Second Wave. The First Korean Wave, that began in the mid-1990s, was led by Korean TV dramas and was largely limited to Asia. The Second Korean Wave, starting from the early 2010s, has extended to other parts of the globe. In the era of the Second Korean Wave, K-pop is spearheading the transnational diffusion of Korean culture (Kim Y, 2013).

This chapter explores the two phases of the Korean Wave by identifying major cultural contents that became very popular outside South Korea. It also examines spill-over effects of the Korean Wave on South Korea's economy.

The First Korean Wave

The First Korea Wave began in 1997 with the national China Central Television (CCTV) airing the Korean drama *What is Love*? With "the second-highest ratings ever in the history of Chinese television" (Shim 2006:28), the drama was so popular that CCTV aired it several times. Soon, more K-dramas were introduced. Some very popular K-dramas, aired in China and Hong Kong, include: *A Wish Upon a Star* (1998), *Stars in My Heart* (1999), the *Endless Love* Series, *Winter Sonata* (2002) *Autumn in My Heart* (2003) and *Daejanggeum: Jewel in the Palace* (2003). In Hong Kong, *Daejanggeum*, a historical K-drama, was tremendously popular as its viewing rate remained around 47%.

In addition to TV dramas, starting from the late 1990s, Chinese radio stations and regional music television channels including Channel V and Star TV began broadcasting Korean pop music videos (Jung SK 2014).

By the early 2000s, the Korean Wave spread to other parts of Asia. In the Philippines, the Korean Wave began with a TV drama, *Autumn in My Heart* (2003). Afterwards, it was followed by other K-dramas including *Endless Love, Winter Sonata,* and *Stairway to Heaven, Full House,* and *Daejanggeum* (Igno and Cenidoza 2016). As for Japan, the Korean Wave began in the early 2000s with NHK airing the Korean drama *Winter Sonata* in 2003. The drama was so popular that Bae Young-Jun (called Yon-sama in Japan), the male lead in *Winter Sonata*, became a national celebrity in Japan. Even the former Japanese prime-minister Junichiro Koizumi said during the 2004 Parliamentary election: "I'll make great efforts so that I will be as popular as Yon-sama and be called Jun-sama" (Kozhakhmetova, 2012).

With the initial success of the Korean TV dramas above, demands for Korean entertainment products sharply increased in many parts of Asia (Japan, China, Hong Kong, Taiwan, Vietnam, Malaysia, and Indonesia) (Jung and Hirata 2012). More importantly, people's interests in other Korean cultural contents also increased. Between 2008 and 2010, more than three million copies of a Korean comic book series, *The Survival Series* were sold in China, while the numbers for Taiwan, Thailand, and Japan were two million, 1.5 million, and half a million respectively (Oh and Park 2012). Against this backdrop of the Korean Wave, other Korean cultural products such as video games and K-pop made an inroad into Asian markets. In Thailand, together with the success of early TV dramas, K-pop acts such as Se7en and Rain became popular in the mid-2000s (Siriyuvasak and Shin 2007).

The popularity of Korean TV dramas spread to Latin America mainly via YouTube and with some help from Korean governmental bodies and corporations. Starting with the 2002 World Cup in South Korea, governmental organizations such as embassies and cultural associations distributed Korean cultural contents to TV broadcasting companies in some Latin American countries either for no charge or for nominal fees. Starting with Peru's national television network airing *Star in my heart* and *Daejanggeum,* about twenty Korean dramas had been broadcasted by the end of 2000s (Ko et.al. 2014).

K-dramas were introduced to some countries in the Middle East and East Europe. As table 9.1 shows, numerous K-dramas became very popular in the Middle East. In particular, *Jumong*, a Korean historical TV drama series, was a mega hit in Iran and Turkey. It was reported that, when the drama was aired, traffic volumes in Teheran were significantly reduced because people stayed home to watch the drama. Some major Arabic TV channels such as Dubai TV aired some Korean TV dramas. After the Korean TV drama *My Lovely Sam-soon* became a big hit in Israel in 2006, more than 30 K-dramas were broadcasted in Israel (Otmazgin and Lyan, 2014).

Table 9.1 Popular K-dramas during the First Korean Wave (1997-2010)

Coffee shop prince (2007), Star in my heart (1997), Boys over Flowers (2009), My lovely Sam-soon (2005), Daejanggeum, Sunggwingwan scandal (2010), Winter Sonata (2002), Full House, Jumong (2007), My sassy girl (2001), What is love (1992), Autumn in my heart (2000), All about Eve (2000), All In (2003)

By the late 2000s, the Korean Wave spread to some parts of Eastern Europe. Starting with *Daejanggeum* (The Jewel of the Palace), the main Romanian public television channel (TVR1) has broadcasted more than a dozen K-dramas in 2009 (Marinescu and Balica, 2013).

The Second Korean Wave

Compared to the First Korean Wave which largely relied on Korean TV dramas, the Second Korean Wave has been led by the rising popularity of K-pop. The unprecedented enthusiastic reception of K-pop stars by European fans at the "SM Town Live World Tour" concert (held in Paris) surprised mainstream French media in 2012. The French newspaper, Le Monde, reported the European fans' explosive response with attention grabbing headlines such as "Korean Wave Strikes Europe" while another French newspaper, Le Figaro, used similar headlines entitled, "The Korean Wave Hits Zenith".

Capitalizing on the popularity of K-pop, many TV dramas were made specifically to appeal to K-pop fans. Such dramas include *Dream High* and *Hwarang* which heavily featured prominent K-pop artists. IU (South Korea's most popular singer-songwriter), some members of 2PM and Miss A, as well as Park Jin-young, the founder of JYP, starred in *Dream High.* The drama tells a fictional story about a group of high school students who face many challenges in their pursuit for K-pop stardom. *Hwarang*, a historical TV drama aired in 2016, featured several well-known K-pop idols including BTS' V, the boyband ZE:A's Park Hyung-sik and SHINee's Minho. The drama depicts a fictional story of love and friendship among members of an elite worrier group, *Hwarang*, set in the time period of the Silla Kingdom (57 BC-AD 935) in Korea.

Table 9.2 Popular K-dramas during the Second Wave

Healer (2014), Dream High (2011), City Hunter (2011), Secret Garden (2011), The Rooftop Prince (2012), My Love from the Stars (2014), Heirs (2013), Six Dragons Flying, She was pretty (2015), Pinocchio (2014), Hwarang (2016), Descendants of the Sun (2016), The Legend of the Blue Sea (2016), Reply 1988 (2016), The K2 (2016), Emergency Couple (2014), My Love from the star (2013), Three Days (2014), Uncontrollably Fond (2016)

In tandem with the rising interests in K-pop, people's interests in other Korean cultural products such as TV dramas continue to rise in many parts of the globe. Some TV dramas attracted millions and billions of views in China.

Aired in 2014, the K-drama, *3 Days*, received more than 300 million views on China's Youku video site (Shin, D 2014). Aired in 2016, the K-drama, *Uncontrollably Fond* (which featured Suzy from K-pop act, Miss A), garnered more than 4.1 billion views on Youku. (Straits Times, 27 February 2017; South China Morning Post, 2 March 2018). Another K-drama, *Descendants Of The Sun*, aired via iQIYI, another Chinese online video service, received close to 4.4 billion views (Straits Times, 27 February 2017). The drama was also aired on Hong Kong's local channel Viu TV. Baidu purchased the drama for $250,000 per episode which equals to almost 40% of the cost of the drama production. The drama became the most-watched show on Viu's K-drama streaming site Viu.com (Forbes Apr 5,

2016). The Korean romantic comedy series *My Love From the Star* was also a big hit in Asia.

Aside from K-dramas, Korean TV variety shows such as *Running Man* and *Knowing Brothers* are widely popular in Asian and other parts of the globe. Most TV shows regularly feature K-pop stars. For instance, Super Junior's Hee-chul is one of the main MCs for *Knowing Brothers.* Another popular TV reality show is *Running Man* in which Korean celebrities compete in various challenging games. Within a day of the release of *Running Man's* most recent episode, K-drama fans around the world upload it on YouTube or Youku (Chinese video-streaming site) with free subtitles in their languages (English, French, Spanish, Chinese, Thai, Malay, Vietnamese, Indonesian, Arabic, Brazilian Portuguese, Russian and Turkish). Due to the global popularity of *Running Man*, actors such as Tom Cruise and Jacki Chan have appeared on the show to promote their films.

Thanks to the growing popularity of TV variety shows, Korean broadcasting companies have been able to export the show formats abroad. For instance, a Chinese TV station bought the format of *Running Man* to create a Chinse version, entitled *Keep Running*, in 2014. China also bought the format of *Produce 101*, Korea's highly successful K-pop competition show. The Chinese version of *Produce 101* became very popular as it attracted 2.3 billion views for the first four episodes (Yonhap May 28, 2018).

Importers of Korean TV contents include countries across the globe. Turkey bought the format for Korean TV variety shows such as *Hidden Singer* and *We Got Married.* The Netherland imported the format of a Korean reality game show, *The Genius* (Iwabuchi, et.al. 2017). In 2014, American NBC bought the remake rights for the Korean reality show *Grandpa Over Flowers*. As the first American adaptation of Korean variety show, it has been broadcasted as a travel-show entitled, *Better Late Than Never* since 2016 (Zhang 2016).

China is, by far, the largest buyer of Korean TV dramas and variety shows. In addition to *Running Man*, China has bought the formats for many Korean variety shows including *We got married, 2 Days & 1 Night, Super Star K, K-pop Star, Real man, and I'm a singer* (Iwabuchi, et.al., 2017). By the mid 2010s, Korea had replaced the U.S., to become the biggest TV program licence exporter to China. Nearly 72.45% of Korean variety shows on Korean TV channels have been introduced to China (Zhang 2016). In addition, other countries in Asia have bought the remake licence for many Korean dramas including *Hotelier, The Devil, Autumn love story, Temptation of Wife, My Sassy Girl, Full House*, and *War of Money* (Iwabuchi, et.al., 2017).

Starting from 2016, though, South Korea encountered a Chinese boycott of Korean goods and services over a geo-political issue. China strongly opposed Seoul's decision to host the American missile system, the Terminal High Altitude Area Defence (THAAD), in South Korea. Although the official reason for stationing THAAD are missile threats from North Korea, the effectiveness of THAAD in protecting South Korea from North Korea's long-range missiles has been hotly debated and strongly doubted. Beijing argued that the real reason for the THADD deployment was Washington's objective to undermine China's military capabilities with a super-surveillance system embedded in the THAAD. Stating that Seoul's deployment of THADD greatly undermines China's security interests, the Chinese government and an overwhelming majority of Chinese people have taken some punitive measures against South Korea. One of the measures was to boycott Korean cultural products including K-pop and K-dramas. Since China is South Korea's biggest trading partner, such punitive trade measures have hurt South Korea's cultural industry. Many Chinese people, with or without encouragement of the Chinese government, showed their disapproval of Korea's military policy by joining mass boycott of Korean products including Korean cosmetics and package tours to Korea. (Vox, 7 March 2017). A similar ban on Korean cultural contents was applied to social media platforms such as Weibo, the Chinese version of Twitter. Chinese netizens called for boycotts of Korean dramas and K-pop videos on Weibo. According to Xinhua, a Chinese newspaper, about "80 percent of Chinese people would support a ban of South Korean stars appearing in Chinese TV shows" (Vox, 7 March 2017).

The leader of an opposition party, Moon Jae-In, came into power after South Korea's famous "Candlelight Revolution", which lasted between late 2016 and early 2017, led to a peaceful regime change in South Korea (Park, M 2018). Under the new administration led by Moon, Seoul has pursued a different foreign policy compared to the previous corrupt Park administration. The Moon administration has sought to restore peaceful and balanced inter-state relations with its neighboring countries including China and North Korea. As of 2018, there have been many positive signs that the two countries work toward restoring a friendly diplomatic relationship. As a result, many people expect that the ban on Korean cultural contents will be fully lifted in China in the near future.

The Spill-over Effects of the Korean Wave

The rising popularity of K-pop and Korean dramas has produced many spill-over effects in Korea. One of the spill-over effects is the rising interest in Korean language. Since many K-pop fans want to learn Korean language, the enrollment in Korean languages courses at schools and universities has significantly increased. The number of students enrolled in Korean language courses at US universities jumped from 163 in 1996 to 14,000 in 2016 (Pickles 2018).

The enrollment of foreign students at universities in South Korea also increased. As of October 2017, 123,000 foreign students were studying in Korea (Korea Times, April 12, 2018). Many foreign students profess that they became interested in Korean studies because of K-pop. A 22-year-old Swedish student attending Seoul National University in South Korea said that she came to study in South Korea mainly because of K-pop. As she explains: "I would have never been interested in Korea without K-pop. K-pop was like the door that opened up for my visit to Korea. I think most people who have experienced K-pop would want to visit Korea at least once in their lifetime" (Korea Times, Apr 12, 2018).

Aside from academic institutions, K-pop fans seek learning Korean language via online platforms. For instance, a Korean course at the language learning website "Duolingo" has more than 200,000 students since the course was introduced in 2017. Due to the rising demand for Korean language education abroad, the South Korean government now supports about 130 language institutes in 50 countries (Pickles 2018).

The Korean fashion and cosmetic industries have also benefited from the Korean Wave (Kim Y, 2013). In addition, K-pop related stores, selling Korean clothing and cosmetics, have been rising in many parts of Asia (Kim M 2017). In Europe and North America, some K-pop stores have recently popped up in several cities where fans can buy music CDs and other items relating to K-pop stars. "All in K-pop" in Copenhagen (Denmark) and "Daebak K-pop shop" in Frankfurt (Germany) are examples.

South Korea's tourism industry has also greatly benefited from the Korean Wave. K-drama fans like to visit locations where scenes of their favorite dramas were shot. According to the Korean Tourism Organization (KTO), visitors to South Korea increased from five million in 2000 to 14.2 million in 2014 (Kim, M 2017). In 2016, before the Chinese boycott, over 8 million Chinese tourists visited

South Korea (Park JW 2017). Mainly due to people's interests in K-pop and K-dramas, the number of Indonesian visitors to South Korea jumped from 80,000 in 2008 to 230,000 in 2017 (Muchtar 2018). All in all, as shown above, the First and Second Korean Wave, aided by the popularity of K-pop, has produced significant spill-over effects in many areas of Korea's economy.

CHAPTER 10

The Role of Politics, Business, and Culture in K-pop's Development

As for the main reasons for K-pop's global success, previous chapters have identified three factors as the main driving force. They are idiosyncratic elements in K-pop itself, avid K-pop fans, and some innovative music companies in South Korea. Other factors, however, have played an equally important role in fostering the development of South Korea's music industry and K-pop, in particular. They concern political and economic factors as well as technology and culture. This chapter examines South Korea's political landscape that shaped the country's legal frameworks for permissible cultural and economic activities. It discusses the role of politics and business in the development of music industry. It also explores how the interaction between technology, business, and culture has helped to transform K-pop into a global phenomenon.

Political Factors

The democratization of South Korea in the late 1980s has facilitated a positive socio-political environment for South Korea's cultural industry. Until 1987, South Korea was under the rule of quasi-military governments (under the former generals Park Chung-hee and Chun Doo-hwan) that suppressed democracy and civil liberty (Park M 2018). Chun Doo-hwan, after taking power via military coup in 1980, enacted the Basic Press Law to control media, closed down private TV stations, and licensed only two state-run TV channels, KBS and MBC. Korea's music industry and private media outlets were tightly controlled by the government.

Despite political suppression, democratic opposition to Chun's dictatorial regime continued to grow throughout the 1980s (Park M 2018). In 1987, Korea's democratization movement led by students and citizens eventually forced the Chun regime to change the country's national constitution favorable to civil society (Park M 2018).

Under civilian administrations led by Kim Young-sam (1993-1998), Kim Dae-jung (1998-2003), and Roh Moo-hyun (2003-2008), South Korea's political system became gradually liberalized. Political liberalization starting in the 1990s was crucial for creating a social and economic environment conducive to the cultural industry (Shin and Kim, 2013). First, with the repeal of the repressive Press Law, state control on media has loosened and accordingly many TV channels, both local terrestrial channels, and cable and satellite channels, became available. A wide range of radio and television programs further provided venues through which people can enjoy pop music. In addition, starting from 1997, Arirang TV, the Korean English language TV channel, aired music programs such as 'Pops in Seoul Weekly Chart', 'Show Music Tank' and 'Show Biz Extra' for non-Korean speakers.

The other political factor was the role of Korean government in providing the necessary Internet infrastructure for Korea's cultural industries to thrive later in the age of SNS and smartphones. Korea's Internet infrastructure, rapidly developed by the support of the Korean government under Kim Dae-jung in the late 1990s, provided a technological and economic condition conducive to Korea's creative economy. The Kim Dae-jung administration (1998-2003) launched an Internet infrastructure project known as the "Cyber Korea 21 Program" to enhance Korea's digital economy ahead of other countries. Under the program, South Korea saw a massive expansion of Internet infrastructure and as a result, by 2002, South Korea became the most wired country in the world with the world's most extensive broadband penetration (Lie 2014). In this environment where the Korean public in general are savvy of IT technology, from very early on, Korean music professionals and small music companies came to utilize the Internet and digital technology to create and distribute K-pop. The Internet also facilitated the dissemination of K-pop around the world as it no longer exclusively relies on traditional television and radio airtime subject to national regulations.

Another political factor, which helped the innovative music companies, came in the late 1990s. The Kim Dae-jung administration introduced legislations designed to foster the development of small-and-medium size companies by limiting the economic concentration of chaebol (large corporations). In this legislative environment, the three major music agencies, initially all small music studios established in the 1990s, were given a much better chance to compete against Korea's business establishments.

In addition, the Kim Dae-Jung administration made efforts to promote Korea's cultural industry. To this end, it provided $148.5 million funds to the Ministry of Culture and Tourism (MCT). The MCT offered training and educational programs to small-medium size businesses in cultural industry (Kozhakhmetova, 2012). Broadcasting companies and the film industry in South Korea were required to use domestic cultural contents especially from independent producers until the mid-2000s (Rånes 2014). The mandatory quota system of using domestic cultural contents provided time and space for small local producers to develop their quality products before they were thrown into a completely liberalized environment where they had to compete against global counterparts. By the mid-2000s when South Korea entered into a series of free trade agreements with multiple countries including the USA, South Korea had already begun exporting its cultural products including K-dramas and TV programs. South Korea's cultural contents exports increased from US$12.7 million in 1999 to US$1.5 billion in 2007 (Chua 2012, 19).

The administration under Roh Moo-Hyun (2003-2008) made concerted efforts to promote Korean culture abroad. To this end, Korean embassies and other governmental bodies such as cultural organizations sponsored cultural events abroad. Against this backdrop, Korean embassies, for instance, distributed popular Korean TV dramas to Latin American TV stations (Han 2017). The Korean governments since 2008 more or less continued the Korean-culture-promotion policy pursued by their predecessors. Governmental organizations such as embassies and Korean cultural centers have continued to sponsor cultural events such as K-pop festivals.

Technological Factors

South Korea's early adoption of digital technology has provided a socio-economic environment favorable to K-pop's success. The Internet and social media greatly facilitate the global diffusion of K-pop. As a result, the Korean music industry can reap the benefit from the SNS-driven global popularity of K-pop.

Technological factors are crucial for K-pop's global expansion. Instead of relying on traditional TV and radio programs as the main venues for marketing, small and medium sized Korean music agencies have actively utilized YouTube and other video-sharing sites such as Youku and Vline as new strategic outlets for promoting K-pop music at home and abroad. By quickly adopting Internet-based strategies and social media driven marketing, the innovative

Korean music agencies have capitalized on the sale of digitized music.

The global environment of the culture industry has profoundly changed with the rise of smartphones and numerous social networking sites. K-pop fans utilize social networking platforms (e.g., Facebook, Twitter, Instagram, Weibo, Baidu, YouTube, Youku, Vline, Kakao Story, Band, Naver, Daum, etc.) to share K-pop related contents. Almost instant and free access to digitized music and popular cultural contents on YouTube or similar Internet-based portals has allowed unknown music companies to promote their artists in the global market. All three major companies (SM Entertainment, YG Entertainment and JYP Entertainment) have their own YouTube and Youku channels (in English) to promote K-pop contents worldwide (Jung and Hirata 2012).

Nowadays, portable devices for entertainment are ubiquitous. People enjoy watching music videos on their smartphones and tablets. Most South Koreans own smart phones with which K-pop contents are consumed everyday. Similarly, people outside South Korea use smart phones, tabs or PCs to access K-pop music bypassing their local TV and radio stations that do not broadcast K-pop in their countries.

Fan-led YouTube or Youku channels have fueled the dissemination of K-pop as K-pop related contents on YouTube have skyrocketed in the last 10 years. Additionally, many K-pop news web-sites such as *Allkpop, Koreaboo*, and *Soompi* emerged due to growing international interests in K-pop. For instance, *Allkpop* is an US-based Korean pop blog for K-pop news, which has 10 million monthly readers worldwide (Jung 2011). *Soompi* is the publishing division of Japanese Rakuten Viki, a global streaming site for watching Asian entertainment shows.

Economic Factors

The Korean music industry has seen the sale of music jumping from $16.7 million to 277 million in 2013 (Messerlin, 2017). In 2009, the value of the Korean music industry was roughly half the size of the French counterpart but by 2013, South Korea surpassed France with regard to music exports (Messerlin, 2017). In 2016. the global revenue from K-pop alone reached a record of $4.7 billion (Kim S 2017) and one year later, K-pop became a thriving global industry valued more than 5 billion dollars.

Once the K-pop industry started generating profits, other businesses joined in to capitalize on K-pop's rising popularity. Business communities from large corporations to small-and medium size firms, all seek to use K-pop stars to promote their goods and services. As a result, they help to further promote K-pop abroad and reinforce the K-pop industry. It is like a snowballing chain reaction. Once in motion, it becomes bigger and bigger as it attracts other snow particles (businesses in the K-pop case).

The growing number of corporate sponsorship reflects K-pop's global popularity and at the same time, it has the effect of reinforcing the trend of K-pop's global outreach. Korea's large corporations such as Hyundai, Samsung and LG have all become sponsors of K-pop concerts and Korean cultural events abroad. LG sponsored a K-pop dance contest, entitled K-pop LG, in Colombia between 2011 to 2013. In 2012, Samsung sponsored Big Bang's world tour concert (know as the "Big Bang Alive Galaxy Tour" in 13 countries (Han 2017).

Both domestic and foreign companies employ K-pop artists for marketing their businesses as they appear on commercial ads. LG's electronic product, a Bluetooth speaker which the girl group Twice advertised, was "sold out within fifty minutes after it went up for pre-orders" (Jolin 2017). The French jewelry and fashion brand, Agatha Paris, sold out a very pricy suitcase, featuring EXO, "almost immediately after it was launched" (Jolin 2017). Luhan, formerly a member of EXO-M, is frequently featured in commercial ads for luxury brands. In 2016, he became the face of Cartier and worked with the luxury fashion house Louis Vuitton. He also appeared in a commercial for carmaker Lexus (South China Morning Post, 2 March 2018). In 2018, Coca-Cola launched special edition cans and bottles featuring BTS (Tay, 2018). Victoria Song from the girl group F(x), acts as a spokeswoman for the K-beauty brand Tonymoly as well as for luxury jeweller Damiani (South China Morning Post, 2 March 2018). The internationally known cosmetic brand, Lancôme, hired Suzy, a former member of girl group Miss A, to advertise its products in Asia. She also appears in ads for Korean cosmetic companies such as "The Face Shop" (South China Morning Post, 2 March 2018).

Other business players in Korea's tourism and educational industries seek to capitalize on K-pop's popularity. As K-pop led to people's rising interests in Korean culture, many K-pop fans wish to visit Korea or learn Korean language. Against this backdrop, private businesses, together with Korean governmental bodies such as the *Visit Korea* committee and Korail (Korea Railroad cooperation), organize or sponsor Korean cultural events at home and abroad to attract foreign visitors and students (Jolin 2017).

Many media companies also seek to take advantage of the K-pop boom. Koreaboo is a case in point. Founded in 2012, Koreaboo is a digital media company producing news on K-pop stars. With 40 million viewers, Koreaboo operates in six countries including Canada, the UK, Australia, China, and Singapore. Together with CJ E&M (a Korean corporation), Koreaboo co-founded the KCON, an annual Korean pop culture convention and music festival. Since 2012, KCON has been held in many parts of the globe including the

USA, Mexico, Japan, United Arab Emirates, and France. The 2017 KCON was held in more than seven countries attracting more than 200,000 attendees.

Cultural Factors

Aside from the political and economic factors, one more element should be added to the explanation of K-pop's global success. That is a cultural factor. South Koreans have been socialized to sing at social or political gatherings. When you travel South Korea, you will find that Noraebang (private singing room) and Noraebang-gigye (singing machine) are ubiquitous in the country. In 2009, the number of daily users of Noraebang was recorded as 1.9 million (Cho JS, 2011). As of 2014, the total number of Noraebang was estimated to be 40,000, in addition to 2 million Noraebang machine that South Korean citizens own at home (Cho JS, 2014).

Before the introduction of Noraebang in the early 1990s, Koreans used to sing at home as well as in public places such as taverns, plazas or parks. Throughout the 1980s, hundreds and thousands of university students, defying the dictatorial Chun regime, took to streets almost every day. Demanding civil liberty and democracy, protestors chanted slogans and sang political songs. At most social and political gatherings, South Koreans have been socialized to sing collectively (Park, M 2018). In the 1980s, it was quite common that workers and students visited taverns or "soju-jip" (mom-and-pop restaurants selling Korean liquor) after work or study, where they sang together while drinking and socializing. Since the early 1990s, Koreans have been more likely to visit Noraebang as a way of socializing. In this cultural context, it is not surprising that South Korea has many talented singers, composers, and songwriters.

Table 10.1 South Korea's TV music shows including auditions and K-pop survival reality shows

K-pop Star, Idol School, Produce 101, M Countdown, Ingi-gayo, Music Bank, Show me the money, The Unit, After school club, Sixteen, Mix Nine, Show Champion, Roommate, Simply K-pop, Superstar K, Boys 24, Extreme K-pop survival, All the K-pop, Pops in Seoul, MBC Gayo-daejeon, K-pop Star hunt, The Show, Open concert, Show! Music Core, Produce 48, Unpretty Rapstar, Mix & Match, Win: who's next, No Mercy, Pentagon Maker, Finding Momoland, Mydol, The Voice of Korea, Dancing 9, Star Audition, Top Band, Korea's got talent, Peppermint, You and I, KBS Live Music Warehouse, Yoon Do Hyun's loveletter, Jeongook Norae-jarang, Kim Dong Ryul's For You, Kim Jung-eun's Chocolate, Music Travel LaLaLa, Music Space, Music Camp, SBS Music Wave, You Hee-Yeol's Sketchbook, King of Masked Singer

While Koreans love to sing, they also like to listen to talented singers. As table 10.1 shows, South Korea has more than 50 TV music programs (including public auditions and music talent shows) that are related to K-pop alone. In addition to the above music shows, many more TV variety shows such as *Weekly Idol* and *Knowing Brothers* regularly invite K-pop stars as guests. Growing up with these numerous televised music shows, it is understandable that many Korean youngsters, dreaming of becoming the next K-pop star, want to enter into Korea's music industry in their early teens.

CHAPTER 11

A Biased Portrayal of K-pop: Negative Stereotypes of Asians in the "Western" Media

Analysing the success of K-pop, some people, either unintentionally or purposely, spread biased opinions about K-pop and reinforce negative stereotypes of Koreans or Asians in general. This chapter picks on some of the negative publicities concerning K-pop and discusses how a biased representation of K-pop can perpetuate cultural prejudices against Asians. A biased portrayal of K-pop can be manifested in many ways. Some examples are as follows.

Bias 1. K-pop is not an authentic Korean music but a copycat of "Western" music.

Some critics argue that since K-pop is heavily influenced by "Western music" styles such as hip-hop and rap, K-pop is not a unique Korean music but just a copy cat of western music. For instance, in *K-Pop: Popular Music, Cultural Amnesia, and Economic Innovation in South Korea*, John Lie, asserts that "K-pop is utterly lacking in authenticity, autonomy, and originality" (Lie 2014). His assertion reveals his own bias toward Korean culture as he reifies a national culture. It also reveals his lack of understanding the world history of cultures.

Why is hip-hop or rap regarded as a "Western" music genre? Why not "African" music? Both hip-hop and rap were originally developed in the 1970s by African-Americans in urban ghettos in the USA. As hip-hop or rap music became popular in North America, the style was adopted by musicians all around the world. When British or French people produce hip-hop songs, almost no one asserts that their music is not authentic because they are heavily influenced by the African-American music style. Almost no one claims that American or British music is "Africanized". They simply remain part of "Western" music traditions. Here, the notion of "the West" is heavily overloaded with culturally biased meanings.

From this example, one can identify that many layers of problematic assumptions exist behind the notion of the West. First, the category of the West functions to equate the USA with its political allies in Europe and some of former British colonies such as Canada and Australia. The category of the West, thus, erases internal cultural differences within the countries supposedly belonging to the West. Secondly, the category of the West functions to denote some people that have been labelled as the "white race" or "Caucasians". Even if African-Americans first developed hip-hop, rap, Jazz, and Soul music, their music was simply labelled as "Western" and added to the cultural heritage stock of the "white race" or the "West". In contrast, when musicians outside the "West" adopt hip-hop, R&B, or rap, their cultural product is regarded as a non-authentic copycat of the Western music. Thereby, the West, as a politically loaded category, reinforces the pervasive mis-informed notion that people outside the West are culturally (also economically, politically, and technologically) lagging and that they are always in the perpetual process of catching up with the West by imitating what the West has been doing.

Bias 2. K-pop stars are manufactured.

Some critics argue that K-pop stars are not genuine artists because they play no creative role in producing music. As Lie argues:

> There may be exceptions, but K-pop performers in general, *unlike American stars*, did not start out playing music in the family garage or composing songs in their bedrooms. Instead, they auditioned and were trained to be performers. In the K-pop studio system, perspiration is worth more than inspiration. The K-pop system is testament to the power of training over genius. (Lie 2014)

Here, too, one can see the reinforced notion of the West's cultural superiority by deliberately contrasting Korean artists with American counterparts. Surely, some K-pop stars play no role in the creation of their songs, but the same applies to performing artists in other countries. What is missing in the above narrative about K-pop stars is that South Korea has many creative K-pop artists who can compose and write their own music. To name just a few, they include most members of popular K-pop acts as Big Bang, BTS, Block B, SHInee, and SEVENTEEN. The full list of all K-pop stars who have produced their own albums and singles is very long! One should not simply brush off the talented K-pop stars as a mere exception!

Downplaying creativity and musicality of K-pop artists, some critics stress the Korean training system of K-pop stars as the main reason for its success. As Lie put it:

> As for autonomy, K-pop stars, by and large, only sing and dance. They execute what has been conceived for them; they wear what they are told to wear, they sing what they are told to sing, and they move and behave as

> they are told to move and behave. For this reason, some critics deride K-pop performers as robots because they seem to lack artistic autonomy and personal will. (Lie 2014)

Here, K-pop is portrayed not as an art but as a mass-produced, standardized entertainment product. In such a negative narrative, Koreans are likened to faceless masses, lacking individuality and free will and K-pop stars are portrayed as people akin to well-trained but disposable service workers. Such a portrayal affirms a stereotypical image of Asians who are "generally known to work hard throughout their lifetime" (Kwon EJ 2017) but lack creativity and autonomy.

It is true that label companies play a crucial role in producing music and training K-pop stars. It might be also true that some creative singers are pressured to give up their own music style, if it conflicts with preferences of their companies. This should not be taken as a sign of K-pop stars lacking creativity. Similar cases can be equally found in other countries.

What is not obvious at first and therefore troubling is the fact that the narrative about K-pop stars' supposed lack of musicality and autonomy is deeply influenced by cultural biases against Asians. Table 11.1 identifies some pervasive stereotypes that function to empower the "West" at the expense of the others. Similar denigrating narratives can be heard from other arguments about K-pop.

Bias 3. K-pop is South Korea's manufactured product for export.

Some journalists and scholars circulate an argument that K-pop acts are corporate commodities and that the global success of K-pop is largely due to aggressive export policies of the Korean government and corporations. Such narratives can be found in numerous European and American media outlets including BBC, The Guardian, and The New York Times.

The New York Times, for instance, carried an article about the K-pop boyband, Big Bang, back in 2015. Comparing K-pop to automobiles, the article argues that as in the case with car exports, South Korea copied the boyband music format from the US and now exports a copycat (that is, Big Bang) to the USA (Kwon EJ 2017). As the article reads,

> "Boy bands are an industry and aesthetic all but abandoned by the American pop machine. But like, say, automobiles, South Korean success with the form is another example of a concept kick-started here but perfected elsewhere. A night with Big Bang is a loud reminder that American exceptionalism is waning — long live imports, though." (New York Times, October 12, 2015)

The above article closely echoes some pervasively negative opinions about the K-pop industry among journalists in Europe and North America. For instance, a reaction video "YouTuber react to K-pop", which garnered more than 22,6 million views, circulates the same view that Korean corporations "train" and "pump out" K-pop groups "constantly" as a commodity to export. Comparing K-pop with American pop, some YouTubers commented that such Korean practice is "creepy" or "bizarre".

Table 11.1 Cultural Stereotypes Empowering the West

The West	The Rest (Asia, Africa, the Middle East, South America)
Creative/ artistic/ original	Imitating / Standardized

Autonomous individual	Undifferentiated, faceless masses/ a collective/ a unified group
Leader / Inventors / Pathfinders	Followers
Innovative thinking	Conformative / Traditional/ conservative
Human rights/ Respect and value individuals	Value institutions and authority more than individual rights
Democracy and Freedom	Dictatorship and Suppression

As shown, the "Western" media tend to frame the success of K-pop in a denigrating or alarming manner. They describe K-pop's success mainly due to an aggressive export policy of the Korean government and Korean corporations. What is notable is the absence of similar claims about American or "Western" music. Almost no journalists or scholars question the profit motivations of American music companies or the American government's support for the diffusion of American culture abroad. Most people do not question why people all around the world listen to American songs although many do not understand English! But if non-Koreans listen to K-pop, it becomes an enigma for some people and they look for some dark forces in operation behind K-pop's rise to a global fandom.

All in all, those negative narratives deprive K-pop artists of agency and power by describing them as passive masses to be treated like commodities or exploitable employees by some greedy Korean corporations. By denigrating K-pop as one of many export items pushed by the Korean government and corporations, they tend to conjure up the image of the West being flooded with cheap copycats coming from Asia. Such a perspective is completely in sync with the mainstream political narratives in the "West" that China and other Asian countries are accused of stealing technologies from "the West" to manufacture cheap copycats for exports.

Musicianship of Creative K-pop Artists: A Short List

As discussed throughout the book, there are abundant examples to contradict some persistent biases against K-pop. Contrary to the claims about the lack of musicianship, numerous K-pop artists compose and write their own songs as well as for others. As a K-pop observer notes,

> the "record labels in Korea are beginning to churn out more artists who are writing and producing their own songs, and playing instruments. Artist authenticity has never been higher in K-Pop, yet the genre's stereotypes endure in the West" (Kliebhan 2017).

The following is a short-list of K-pop artists who have produced numerous K-pop hits.

Block B

Zico, the leader of Block B, has written and produced many hits. With approximately 100 credits to his name, Zico is one of the most prolific songwriters in South Korea (Koreaboo, 13 December 2017).

B1A4

Jin-young, a member of B1A4, has written, composed and produced most of B1A4's songs including "A Lie," "Sweet Girl," and "Solo Day". He has produced songs for other artists including I.O.I and Oh My Girl.

SHINee

Jonghyun, the late leader of the boy band SHINee, produced many hits for the group as well as for his own albums. Songs to his credits include: "Juliette," "View," and "She Is". He also wrote EXO's "Playboy" and Lee Hi's "Breathe (Koreaboo, 13 December 2017).

Mino, a member of SHINee, has also contributed to the creation of the band's songs.

Pentagon

Several members of the ten-member boyband, Pentagon, have composed and written most of the groups' singles. The contributors include: E'Dawn, Hui, Hongseok, Kino, Yuto, Jinho, and Wooseok. In particular, E'Dawn and Hui,are the two main artists who have most contributed to the production of the group's albums.

BTS

All members of BTS are involved in the production of their own music. Among them, RM (Rap Monster), Suga and J-Hope are the most active members with regard to writing and composing songs. They helped to create many BTS' hits including "Save Me" and "Blood, Sweat & Tears". In addition to producing for the band, RM writes songs for others including Homme's (a group under Big Hit) single, "Dilemma".

Akdong Musician

Lee Chan-hyuk, the male vocalist of Akdong Musician, has composed and written most songs on their albums.

CNBLUE

Jung Yong-hwa, the leader of CNBLUE, has over 100 writing credits. He helped to write almost all of the band' songs as well as for others.

Big Bang

All of Big Bang members have participated in the production of their own music. Especially, GD, T.O.P., and Taeyang have an extensive repertoire of songs that they have written and composed for the group.

Highlight

Yong Jun-hyung has co-written most of Highlight's songs including "Shock," "Fiction," "Good Luck," and "Plz Don't Be Sad." In addition, he has helped to create songs for other K-pop groups including Apink, BTOB, EXID, and HyunA.

DAY 6

Like Big Bang and BTS, all of the DAY6 members take part in the writing of their own songs. Among them, Young K is the most active songwriter of the group. He has also helped to create songs for other groups including GOT7 and UP10TION (jadicus35 2017).

iKON

B.I. (the lead rapper of the group) has helped to produce the group's music. Aside from his own group, he also composed tracks for his own albums as well as for others including WINNER and PSY. He has also co-written the lyrics for Black Pink's "Whistle" (Koreaboo, 13 December 2017).

B.A.P

Bang Yong-guk, the lead rapper of B.A.P., has co-written many of the group's tracks, including "Warrior" and "One Shot." He has also composed for other groups including VIXX's "Love Me Do" (jadicus35 2017).

IU

IU is one of the most prolific singer-songwriters in South Korea. She has composed and written numerous songs on her albums including "Twenty-three", "Friday", "Shoes", and "The Shower". In 2017, IU was chosen as the most beloved K-pop artist of the year in South Korea.

2PM

2PM members, Junho and Jun K, produced their own songs. Junho is credited to numerous songs of 2PM and his own solo hits including "Give it to me" and "Set me free". Jun K has written and composed many of the group's hits including "My House" and "Go Crazy" (jadicus35 2017).

And there are many more K-pop artists who create their own music. The list goes on. The point is that they should not be dismissed as a mere exception to the alleged norm (lacking musicianship) in the K-pop industry.

The "Cultural Proximity" & "Cultural Hybridization" Theory Revisited: A Persistent Reification of Culture

Some scholars have suggested that the success of K-pop and the Korean Wave in general are largely due to "cultural proximity" between Korea and other Asian countries. They identify some shared cultural traditions such as Confucian ethics and Buddhism as reasons for the Korean Wave. This "cultural proximity" explanation might be plausible in East Asia but quickly loses its currency in South Asia or in other parts of the globe.

The cultural explanation, however, is hard for some analysts to abandon. Still, Euro-centric views influence some scholars' approach to national culture and K-pop. The "cultural hybridization" theory is a case in point. Some scholars argue that "it is cultural hybridization between Western universalism and Asian exoticism (or particularism) that is pivotal in attracting transnational audiences" (Oh and Park 2012). In the same line of thinking, some scholars even came up with an argument that ethnic minorities (the second and third generations of migrants in Europe and Latin America) are the driving force behind the Korean Wave in Europe. For instance, a Swedish scholar suggests:

> Regarding the non-Western and non-white aspects of hallyu and their connections to the fan base among minority Swedes, it is important to remember that Swedish and Western pop culture and hallyu are very different from each other in terms of gender roles and views on for example violence, sex and drugs as well as on family values and patriarchy and homosexuality. This means that children of Third World migrants from Asia, Africa and South America most probably can recognize themselves more in hallyu than in Swedish and Western pop culture due to its patriarchal and traditional aspects. (Hubinett 2012)

The above assertion reveals a deeply entrenched belief among some people that the "Western" culture, whatever that may signify, is clearly different from the culture of "Third World migrants from Asia, Africa and South America" (Hubinett 2012). For many, the Western culture is the culture of the "white race", while all other cultures belong to the culture of "Third World" and of other "races". Making a racialized argument about culture, Hubinett further asserts that "white" fans in Europe are attracted to K-pop only because it was somewhat "de-Koreanized" or "whitened". As he put it:

> the idealising of white body ideals which is so common in hallyu seems to have an appeal both to white and non-white Swedes alike, although this appeal probably derives from different desires and identifications. The whitening of Korean bodies and the relative "odourless" of hallyu in terms of de-Koreanisation and Westernisation can be appealing to white fans, and also to non-white fans, as both groups tend to idealise whiteness. However, the whitening of hallyu may also

> make it less appealing to white fans who are actively seeking something which is non-Western, Asian and exotic, and it may also discard non-white fans who will not be able to identify with the whitened bodies of hallyu. (Hubinett 2012)

The above statement is downright offensive to Koreans and anyone who does not belong to "the West"! Why such an assertion is offensive will become evident, if we take Hollywood movies and American pop as an example to compare. Most people do not ask why Hollywood movies and American pop enjoy global popularity. Most people don't ask why people outside the US consume American cultural products. Is it because people outside the USA feel some kind of cultural affinity with Americans, or is it because they look for some exotic, American (or "Western"), elements? For instance, in Germany, one can hear American pop songs everywhere in cafes, pubs, and on radio programs. One might ask why Germans listen to American pop songs, although many do not understand the English lyrics. Is it because Germans seek something "exotic"? But since Germans belong to "the West", according to the cultural approach, they listen because they must feel some cultural affinity with American (another Western) culture! Since American culture is quite often used interchangeably with "Western culture" or the "white race", one can replace the descriptive term, the American, with the terms like the Western or the white. Then, the following questions may appear quite ridiculous to most people. Why do non-Western people consume "Western" cultural products? Should the Western culture be de-Westernized to appeal to non-Westerners? Will the darkening of "Western" culture appeal to "non-white" fans? Although almost no one raises such questions, the racializing questioning with regard to K-pop is considered to be plausible and even scientific!

Moving away from racialized cultural explanations for K-pop and the Korean Wave, this book has explored multiple societal factors. It has suggested that the popularity of K-pop has been largely shaped by the confluence of numerous societal factors including political and economic factors (see chapter 10), passionate global fan communities (chapter 6), as well as innovative and experimental music producers (chapter 8) and creative K-pop artists themselves (chapter 8 and 11).

References

Allkpop (3 September 2017) Most popular K idols and groups in ur region? https://www.allkpop.com/forum/threads/most-popular-k-idols-and-groups-in-ur-region.98783/page-2

Allkpop (4 July 2018) Kpop Japan Fan club Chart! https://www.allkpop.com/forum/threads/kpop-japan-fan club-chart.192516/

Allkpop (6 June 2017) Which group took the win at this year's 'K-Pop Cover Dance Festival'? https://www.allkpop.com/article/2017/06/which-group-took-the-win-at-this-years-k-pop-cover-dance-festival

Allkpop (July 29, 2018) Chinese rankings reveal which K-Pop idol groups have the biggest fandom in China. https://www.allkpop.com/article/2018/07/chinese-rankings-reveal-which-k-pop-idol-groups-have-the-biggest-fandoms-in-china

Allkpop (May 2, 2018) Weibo KPop Group Rankings. https://www.allkpop.com/forum/threads/weibo-kpop-group-rankings.169118/

ARA (21 September 2018) BTS ARMY https://aminoapps.com/c/btsarmy/info/

Benjamin, Jeff (2013) Girls' Generation Reacts to YouTube Music Awards Win, Talks New Music: Exclusive. *Billboard.* https://www.billboard.com/articles/columns/k-town/5778185/girls-generation-reacts-to-youtube-music-awards-win-talks-new-music

Benjamin, Jeff (2017) “Inside BTS Mania a day in the life of the K-pop superstars”. *Rolling Stone.* https://www.rollingstone.com/music/features/inside-bts-mania-a-day-in-the-life-of-the-k-pop-superstars-w514229

Beyond Hallyu (2012) 12 K-pop Producers and Composers You Should Know. *Beyond Hallyu*. http://beyondhallyu.com/k-pop/12-k-pop-producers-composers-know/

Billboard (13 March 2018) "K-Pop Icons BIGBANG Walk the 'Flower Road' In Final Single Before Hiatus". By Tamar Herman, *Billboard*.

Billboard (17 January 2018) "BTS Hits 12 Million Followers on Twitter". By Tamar Herman. *Billboard.*

Billboard (27 October 2016) "10 Must-Know Facts About K-pop Darlings TWICE". By Tamar Herman. *Billboard.*

Billboard (29 September 2017) "Meet the Fans of BTS: Profiles of American ARMY". *Billboard.* By Tamar Herman.

Billboard (6 March 2018) "Star Wars' Recognizes BTS Fan ARMY As Major Donors of Force For Change UNICEF Campaign". By Tamar Herman. *Billboard.*

Brown, August (2018) KCON aims to ride the 'Korean wave' to pop-culture dominance. *Los Angeles Times*. August 8, 2018.

Cha, E (2017) Big Hit Producer Pdogg Shares What It's Like To Create Music With BTS. *Soompi*. Dec 5, 2017. https://www.soompi.com/article/1089993wpp/big-hit-producer-pdogg-shares-like-create-music-bts

Channel A (4 May 2018) 채널 A [더깊은뉴스]걸그룹만 300 개..데뷔해도 생활고.

Cho, Jae-eun (2011) Sing a song: Noraebang turns 20. *Korea JoongAng Daily*. June 23, 2011.

Cho, Michelle (2017) Domestic Hallyu: K-Pop Metatexts and the Media's Self-Reflexive Gesture. *International Journal of Communication* 11(2017)

Choi Joon-sik (2014) 한국의 예술문화. 21 세기 북스

Choi, Seong-cheol, Xanat Vargas Meza, and Han Woo Park (2014) "South Korean Culture Goes Latin America: Social network analysis of Kpop Tweets in Mexico". *International Journal of Contents*, Volume 10 (1)

CNN (20 September 2017) BTS Rap Monster Interview. https://www.cnn.com/2017/09/20/asia/bts-kpop-rap-monster-interview/index.html)

Cox, Jennifer (2012) "Seoul searching: on the trail of the K-pop phenomenon". *The Guardian*. 28 December 2012.

Cozan (2017) YouKu vs YouTube is the Brand Favorite https://chozan.co/2017/04/13/youku-vs-youtube-why-youku-is-the-brand-favourite/

Danica (2018) "17 Songs Kim Jong Hyun Wrote For SHINee". *Hellokpop*. https://hellokpop.com/kpop/17-songs-kim-jong-hyun-shinee/

DatJoeDoe (2018) Most viewed K-pop music videos in the first 24 hours. *SBS Pop Asia*. 23 May 2018 https://www.sbs.com.au/popasia/blog/2018/05/23/most-viewed-k-pop-music-videos-first-24-hours

Financial Times (23 August 2017) "Korean wave makes a splash worldwide. Last weekend's KCON event in Los Angeles illustrated the power of K-pop". *Financial Times*.

Forbes (15 July 2018) Super Junior's Push Into Latin America Continues The Group's Legacy As Industry Innovators. By Tamar Herman. *Forbes*.

Forbes (18 January 2018) "TWICE Leads JYP Entertainment To Become No. 2 K-Pop Agency". By Tamar Herman. *Forbes*.

Forbes (26 March 2018) "BTS: The K-Pop Group That Finally Won America Over". *Forbes*.

Forbes (April 5, 2016) "Korean Drama 'Descendants of The Sun' Breaks Records Thanks To Chinese Investments". *Forbes*. By John Kang.

Forbes (December 21, 2017) K-Pop Fans Spend Big On Times Square Ads Promoting Their Favorite Stars.

Forbes (June 18, 2018) K-Pop Duo TVXQ! Becomes Best-Selling Foreign Touring Act In Japan. By Tamar Herman.

Forbes (May 26, 2018) BTS's 'Fake Love' Video Hits 100 Million Views In Record Time For K-Pop Group. BY Bryan Rolli

Gogoi, Monami (2017) India knows about EXO, BTS: It's time to acknowledge, K-pop is here to stay. *Hindustan Times*. 10 August 2017.

Guardian (5 June 2018) The A-Z of K-Pop: Know your sasaengs from your monster rookies.

Han, Benjamin (2017) K-Pop in Latin America: Transcultural Fandom and Digital Mediation. *International Journal of Communication* 11

Haynes, Gavin (2018) "Why BTS are the K-pop kings of social media" *The Guardian*. 13 March 2018.

Hemmeke, Katelyn (2017). Planting Rain Forests to Donating Rice: The Fascinating World of K-pop fandom. *Korea Expose*. https://www.koreaexpose.com/fascinating-world-k-pop-fandom-culture/

Heytoto (2016) "7 Choreographers Who Are Dominating K-Pop In 2016". *Soompi*. August 17, 2016.

https://www.soompi.com/article/887131wpp/7-choreographers-making-splash-2016

Hi Chad (July 24, 2018) BLACKPINK DDU-DU DDU-DU reaction! First time watching K-POP! https://www.youtube.com/watch?v=-fRrjVTe1zA

Hicap, Jonah (2018) BTS' DNA becomes most viewed K-pop group music video of all time. *Metro*. 23 April 2018.

Hong Dam-young (2018) S.M. Entertainment to hold K-pop auditions in 10 countries. *The Korea Herald*. January 4, 2018.

Hubinett, Tobias (2012) The Reception and Consumption of Hallyu in Sweden: Preliminary Findings and Reflections. *Korea Observer*. Vol. 43, No. 3, pp. 503-525.

Huffington Post (November 22, 2017) K-Pop Group BTS Broke A World Record. Everything BTS touches turns to gold.

Hunt, Ellen (2018) K-pop Party review: JJCC and Boyfriend offer a lesson in painstaking pop. *The Guardian*. 8 February 2018.

Igno, Jay-Ar M. and Marie Cielo E. Cenidoza (2016) Beyond the "Fad": Understanding Hallyu in the Philippines. *International Journal of Social Science and Humanity*, Vol. 6, No. 9, September 2016

Ilmare42 (2018) Super Junior's Fans E.L.F Win Billboard's 2018 Fan Army Face-Off. *Soompi*. August 29, 2018. https://www.soompi.com/article/1222197wpp/super-juniors-fan-e-l-f-wins-billboards-2018-fan-army-face-off

Iwabuchi, et.al., (2017) Routledge Handbook of East Asian Popular Culture. Routledge.

jadicus35 (2017) 18 K-Pop Idol Songwriters Who Know How To Write A Bop. *Soompi*. August 10, 2017.

https://www.soompi.com/2017/08/10/18-k-pop-idol-songwriters-know-write-bop/

Jolin, Johan Williams (2017) The South Korean Music Industry. The Rise and Success of 'K-Pop'. Bachelor's Thesis. Stockholm University. Department of Asian, Middle Eastern and Turkish Studies

Jung and Hirata (2012) Sun Jung, Yukie Hirata, K-pop Idol Girl Group Flows in Japan in the Era of Web 2.0. *Conflicting Desires*. Volume 12, Issue 2.

Jung, Soo keung (2014) "Global Audience Participation in the Production and Consumption of Gangnam Style." Thesis, Georgia State University. Department of Communication.

Jung, Sun (2011). "K-pop, Indonesian Fandom, and Social Media." In "Race and Ethnicity in Fandom," edited by Robin Anne Reid and Sarah Gatson, special issue, *Transformative Works and Cultures,* no. 8.

Kang, J (2017) Jennifer M. Kang (2017) Rediscovering the idols: K-pop idols behind the mask, *Celebrity Studies*, 8:1, 136-141

Karolina (2016) "BTS Is Inviting You To Join Their Official A.R.M.Y Global Fan club." *KMUSIC*. February 17, 2016. http://officiallykmusic.com/bts-inviting-join-official-r-m-y-global-fan club/

KBIZOOM (March 2018) "Top 10 biggest fan clubs of KPOP artists in China 2018", *KBIZOOM*, https://kbizoom.com/top-10-kpop-groups-china-march-2018

Khachatryan, Lilit (2017) The Rise of Korean Culture Through Media. BA Thesis. American University of Armenia

Khaleej Times (October 31, 2017) Top things you need to know about BTS now. By Samar Khouri.

https://www.khaleejtimes.com/wknd/entertainment/top-things-you-need-to-know-about-bts-now

Kim, Sohee (2017) The $4.7 Billion K-Pop Industry Chases Its 'Michael Jackson Moment'. *Bloomberg*. August 22, 2017.

Kim, Suk-young (2016) The Many Faces of K-pop Music Videos: Revues, Motown, and Broadway in "Twinkle" *The Journal of Popular Culture*, Vol. 49, No. 1

Kim, Yeojin (2013) A Possibility of the Korean Wave. Renaissance Construction through K-Pop: Sustainable Development of the Korean Wave as a Cultural Industry, *36 Hastings Communications and Entertainment Law Journal.* 59 (2013)

Kliebhan, TJ (2017) "In the Processed World of K-Pop, Gifted Songwriters Finally Begin to Emerge". *Paste Magazine*. September 7, 2017.
https://www.pastemagazine.com/articles/2017/08/k-pop.html

Ko, Nusta Carranza, Song No, Jeong-Nam Kim, Ronald Gobbi Simões. (2014) Landing of the Wave: Hallyu in Peru and Brazil. *Development and Society*. Volume 43 (2)

KOFICE (29 January 2018) 인터뷰] 태국 한류 1 세대, 슈퍼주니어 팬클럽 대표 '꿍'과 '짜'를 만나다. 한국 국제문화교류진흥원.
http://kofice.or.kr/c30correspondent/c30_correspondent_02_view.asp?seq=15079

Korea Gallup (2017) 2017 년 올해를 빛낸 가수와 가요 - 최근 11 년간 추이, 아이돌 선호도 포함. 19 December 2017.
http://www.gallup.co.kr/gallupdb/reportContent.asp?seqNo=886

Korea Herald (August 5, 2014) EXO-L website crashed due to heavy traffic.

Korea Times (18 September 2018) K-pop boy band BTS agency under fire for working with Japanese producer Yasushi Akimoto.

Korea Times (Apr 12, 2018) K-pop craze stirs fan migration. Number of foreign students soars as K-pop goes global. By Kang Hyun-kyung.

Koreaboo (11 May 2018) 10 Ridiculously Expensive K-Pop MVs That Cost A Fortune To Make. https://www.koreaboo.com/lists/10-ridiculously-expensive-kpop-mvs-cost-fortune-make/

Koreaboo (13 December 2017) 7 Idols Who Are The Next Top Composers Following G-Dragon https://www.koreaboo.com/buzz/7-idols-who-are-the-next-top-composers-following-gdragon/

Koreaboo (April 22, 2017) The Most Popular Korean Idols In China According To Weibo. https://www.koreaboo.com/news/popular-korean-idols-china-according-weibo/

Koreaboo (March 18, 2015) K-pop fanfiction community ranks as one of the largest in the world. https://www.koreaboo.com/news/k-pop-fanfiction-community-ranks-as-one-of-the-largest-in-the-world/

Koreaboo (March 9th, 2017) ARMY Successfully Promote BTS Through European Radio stations. *Koreaboo.com* https://www.koreaboo.com/stories/chinese-father-23-year-search-kidnapped-daughter/

Koreaboo (May 22, 2018) Chinese ARMYs Launch Biggest BTS Promotion Project Ever.https://www.koreaboo.com/news/chinese-armys-launch-biggest-bts-promotion-project-ever/

Kozhakhmetova, Dinara (2012) "Soft Power of Korean Popular Culture in Japan: K-Pop Avid Fandom in Tokyo". LUND University. Master's Programme in Asian Studies.

Kpop College (2018) Seoul Music High school. https://www.kpopcollege.com/seoul-music-high-school

KpopEurope (December 12, 2014) K-pop Fan clubs and K-pop Related Pages in Europe. http://www.kpopeurope.eu/kpop-fanclubs-in-europe/?lang=en

KpopStarz (November 26, 2014) Girl Group T-ARA Surpass 8 Million Views On Chinese Video Site Youku With 'Little Apple'

Kprofiles (2018) Kpop & K celebrities Profiles. https://kprofiles.com/exo-members-profile/

Kwon, Eun Jee (2017) Korean Wave: Discourse Analysis on Korean Popular Culture in UK and US Digital Newspaper. MA Thesis submitted to Rauboud University

lahkim (2016) 9 Fanfictions Every K-Pop Fan Has To Read. *Soompi*. June 9, 2016. https://www.soompi.com/2016/06/09/10-fanfictions-every-k-pop-fan-has-to-read/

Lee Lee (August 2017) Top 10 most viewed K-pop music videos of all time. *SBS Pop Asia*. 18 August 2017. https://www.sbs.com.au/popasia/blog/2017/08/15/top-10-most-viewed-k-pop-music-videos-all-time

Lee, Lee (2017) 6 female K-Pop choreographers that slay. *SBS Pop Asia*. 3 Mar 2017. https://www.sbs.com.au/popasia/blog/2017/03/03/6-female-k-pop-choreographers-slay

Lie, John. (2014) *K-Pop: Popular Music, Cultural Amnesia, and Economic Innovation in South Korea*. Berkeley: University of California Press

Lifson, Samantha Marie (2016) Chen Shares Which EXO Members Are Most Popular In China And Korea. *KpopStarz* February 29, 2016.

Mare-Sensei (2017) Top 10 Best K-Pop Boy Groups of 2017 https://spinditty.com/genres/Top-10-Best-K-Pop-Boy-Group

Marinescu, Valentina and Ecaterina Balica (2013) Korean Cultural Products in Eastern Europe: A Case Study of the K-Pop Impact in Romania". *Region: Regional Studies of Russia, Eastern Europe, and Central Asia,* Volume 2, Number 1

Messerlin, Patrick A (2017) The Success of k-pop. How Big and Why So Fast? *Asian Journal of Social Science* 45

Muchtar, Joy (2018) Hallyu: Surfin' the Korean Wave in Indonesia. *Jakarta Globe*. 8 May 2018.

My Music Taste (August 26, 2016) We are T International Club. https://blog.mymusictaste.com/blog/2016/08/26/fan club-spotlight-t-international-fan-club-tvxq

Nature1010 (2018) Lee Soo Man, Park Jin Young, And Yang Hyun Suk's Company Stock Values Continue To Show Strong Performance. *Soompi.* July 29, 2018.

New York Times (October 12, 2015) Review: Big Bang, Following the K-pop Playbook with Flash.

Noh, Gwang-woo (2015) 유튜브와 케이팝 팬의 트리뷰트 활동 Youtube and K Pop fan's Tribute Activity. 고려대학교 정보문화연구소.한국콘텐츠학회논문지 '15 Vol. 15 No. 6

Oh, David C (2017) K-Pop Fans React: Hybridity and the White Celebrity-Fan on YouTube. *International Journal of Communication* 11

Oh, Ingyu and Gil-sung Park (2012) From B2C to B2B: Selling Korean Pop Music in the Age of New Social Media. *Korea Observer*. Vol. 43, No. 3.

Otmazgin, Nissim and Irina Lyan (2014) Hallyu across the Desert: K-pop Fandom in Israel and Palestine. *Cross-Currents: East Asian History and Culture Review*, Volume 3, Number 1

Park, Ju-won (2017) K-pop to WeChat: S. Korean Start-ups Want Chinese Tourists. *Korea Expose*, December 13, 2017 https://www.koreaexpose.com/korea-start-up-chinese-tourists-tourism-kpop-wechat/

Park, Jin-hai (2014) America tops the list with 464 'Hallyu' fan clubs. *The Korea Times*. January 9, 2014.

Park, Mi (2018) *South Korea's Candlelight Revolution. The Power of Plaza Democracy*. Coal Harbour Publishing

Peterson, Jacques (2017) "With this award, TWICE can never be shaded again"! *SBS Pop Asia*. https://www.sbs.com.au/popasia/blog/2017/12/06/twice-are-officially-queens-and-they-have-award-prove-it

Pickles, Matt (2018) K-pop drives boom in Korean language lessons. BBC. 11 July 2018. https://www.bbc.com/news/business-44770777

PKCI (2018) Philippine Kpop Committee, Inc. http://pkci.org

Power, John (2016) K-pop Academies. https://mashable.com/2016/02/29/kpop-academies/?europe=true

Rånes, Brian Christer Nebb (2014) Chocolate, Mustard and a Fox. Norwegian K-Pop, Its Production and performance. Master's thesis in Musicology. Norwegian University of Science and Technology.Faculty of Humanities, Department of Music

Romano, Aja (2018) How K-pop became a global phenomenon. *Vox*. February 26, 2018,

Rowe, Jara (2016) 6 of the Hottest Kpop Dance Choreographers. *Fancurve*. March 25, 2016. http://www.funcurve.com/music/6-of-the-hottest-kpop-dance-choreographers/

SBS Pop Aisa (23 May 2018) 7 K-pop idols who choreograph too. 23 May 2018 https://www.sbs.com.au/popasia/blog/2018/05/23/7-k-pop-idols-who-choreograph-too

SBS Pop Asia (30 August 2018) Super Junior fans win Billboard's Fan-Army Face-Off 2018. https://www.sbs.com.au/popasia/blog/2018/08/30/super-junior-fans-win-billboards-fan-army-face-2018

SBS PopAsia (10 November 2017) 8 K-pop Idols and groups who are popular in China. By DatJoeDoe.

SBS PopAsia (26 April 2017) WOW, that's a lot of registered EXO-Ls in less than 3 years! https://www.sbs.com.au/popasia/blog/2017/04/26/exos-official-fan club-hits-huge-membership-milestone

Shim Woo-hyun (2018) BTS world tour sold out. *Asia One*. http://www.asiaone.com/entertainment/bts-world-tour-sold-out

Shin, Diana (2014) SBS Drama '3 Days' Reaches 300 Million Views On Chinese Youku Site. *KpopStarz*. April 28, 2014.

Shin, Solee and Kim Lanu (2013) "Organizing K-Pop: Emergence and Market Making of Large Korean Entertainment Houses, 1980–2010". *East Asia* 30

Sin, Ben (2018) "Inside the K-pop hit machine: how South Korea's music industry has gone global". *South China Morning Post*. 2 April, 2018

Soompi (20 January 2016) K-Pop 101: How to Navigate Fan clubs vs. Fan-cafes. By Harmonicar. https://www.soompi.com/article/807807wpp/k-pop-101-how-to-navigate-fan clubs-vs-fan-cafes

Soompi (January 17, 2015) EXO Voted "Most Popular Asian Group" and "Asia's Best Performance" at the 2014 YOUKU Night. By Magic8289.

Soompi (June 10, 2018) TVXQ Sets New Record In Japan For Foreign Artists With Most Concertgoers At A Single Tour.

South China Morning Post (2 March 2018) "How K-pop stars became the faces of luxury street style in Asia". South China Morning Post

Straits Times (27 February 2017) "Thaad row: China blocks streaming of Korean dramas". *Straits Times*.

Straits Times (4 June 2018) "BTS World Tour Sold Out Nearly Three Months in Advance". *Straits Times*.

Straits Times (31 August 2018) "K-pop girl group Red Velvet to hold first concert in Singapore". *Straits Times*.

Sung, Sang-yeon (2014) K-pop Reception and Participatory Fan Culture in Austria. *Cross-Currents: East Asian History and Culture Review*, Volume 3, Number. 1

Tai, Chrystal (2018) "The K-pop superfans who can make, and break, musical careers in South Korea". *South China Morning Post*. 11 March, 2018

Tan, Marcus (2015) K-Contagion. Sound, Speed, and Space in "Gangnam Style" *TDR: The Drama Review*, Volume 59 (1)

Tay, Vivienne (2018) "Coca-Cola sweetens the deal for K-pop fans with new BTS packaging". July 17, 2018. https://www.marketing-interactive.com/coca-cola-sweetens-the-deal-for-k-pop-fans-with-new-bts-packaging/

Touhami, Batoul (2017) The Influence of the Korean Wave on the Language of International Fans: Case Study of Algerian Fans. *Sino-US English Teaching*, Vol. 14, No. 10

Ubonrat Siriyuvasak & Shin Hyunjoon (2007) Asianizing K-pop: production, consumption and identification patterns among Thai youth, *Inter-Asia Cultural Studies*, 8:1

Vox (7 March 2017) "The surprising reason why China is blocking South Korean music videos and TV". By Lindsay Maizland.

Wilson, Kate (2017) "Rapper T.O.P from K-pop group Big Bang found unconscious after drug overdose". *Straight.* https://www.straight.com/blogra/921371/rapper-top-k-pop-group-big-bang-found-unconscious-after-drug-overdose

Yoon, John (2017) "Top 10 K-Pop Entertainment Companies in South Korea". *Seoul Space.* http://seoulspace.com/2017/08/21/top-10-k-pop-entertainment-companies-in-south-korea/

Zhang, Yuji (2016) Re-examining Herbert Schiller's Cultural Imperialism Thesis with cases of Chinese and Korean Cultural Industries and China's Quest for Soft Power: A Comparative Study of Chinese Film and Online Gaming Industries' Going-out Efforts. MA thesis, Simon Fraser University

Photo Credits

Acrofan.com (2014) Seo Taiji on October 20, 2014. CC-by-3.0. https://commons.wikimedia.org/wiki/File:Seo_Taiji_on_October_20,_2014_(1).jpg

AJEONG JM (2017) BTS receiving a donsang award at the 31st Golden Disk Awards in Seoul on January 14 2017. CC-by-4.0. https://commons.wikimedia.org/wiki/File:BTS_at_the_31st_Golden_Disk_Awards.jpg

BulletProf7BTS (2013) Bangtan Boys at a fan meeting on Music Bank on July 26, 2013. https://commons.wikimedia.org/wiki/File:Bangtan_Boys_at_a_fan meeting_on_Music_Bank_in_July_2013_01.jpg. The photo is licensed under the terms of the cc-by-2.0

DaftTaengk (2017) Wanna One performing at Incheon K-POP Concert on September 9, 2017. CC-by-3.0 https://en.wikipedia.org/wiki/Wanna_One#/media/File:Wanna_One_performing_at_INK_Concert_2017_01.png

Delicato JJ (2017) BLACKPINK performing Playing with Fire at the 31st Golden Disc Awards on January 13, 2017. CC-by-4.0

FBE (2013) YouTubers react to K-pop. https://www.youtube.com/watch?v=ekJ-ldOD0TQ

HeyDay (2016) Red Velvet 2016 in Incheon. CC-by-4.0 https://commons.wikimedia.org/wiki/File:Red_Velvet_Hallyu_Festival_in_Incheon_2016.jpg

How to love (2015) Boy group Infinite on the red carpet of the 24th Seoul Music Awards on January 22, 2015. CC-by-4.0. https://commons.wikimedia.org/wiki/File:Infinite_on_the_red_carpet_of_the_24th_Seoul_Music_Awards_3.jpg

Kamilie (2010) TVXQ CC-by-2.0 https://www.flickr.com/photos/kamilie/5231473494

Kamilie (2011) SHINee. CC-by-2.0. https://www.flickr.com/photos/kamilie/6112845357

Korea.net (2013) EXO at 2013 K-pop World Festival in South Korea. CC-by SA 2.0 https://commons.wikimedia.org/wiki/File:Korea_KPOP_World_Festival_13.jpg

Korean Culture and Information Service (2011) K-pop fans in Egypt. CC-by-2.0. https://commons.wikimedia.org/wiki/File:KOCIS_K-pop_contest_in_Egypt_(6001068528).jpg

LGE (2010) Big Bang members. CC-by-SA-2.0 https://www.flickr.com/photos/lge/4342368094/in/set-72157623383685292

News in Star (2018) Twice at the 2018 Golden Disk Awards CC-by-3.0 https://en.wikipedia.org/wiki/Twice_(band)#/media/File:Twice_on_the_red_carpet_of_the_Golden_Disk_Awards_on_January_10,_2018.png

SM Entertainment (2008) Super Junior at the 1st Asia Tour Concert in 2008. CC-by-4.0 .https://commons.wikimedia.org/wiki/File:Super_Junior_The_1st_Asia_Tour_Concert_2008.jpg

Taehyung's Moment (2014) Bangtan Boys in Hongdae. CC-by-SA 4.0.https://commons.wikimedia.org/wiki/File:Bangtan_Boys_in_Hongdae_on_March_27,_2014.jpg

Ten Asia (2015) GOT7 in a photoshoot for TenAsia Magazine. CC-by-3.0.

https://commons.wikimedia.org/wiki/File:GOT7_Photoshoot_for_TenAsia_Magazine_150920.jpg

TenAsia (2017) BTS at a press conference for the Billboard Music Awards in 2017. CC-by SA 3.0. https://it.m.wikipedia.org/wiki/File:170529_BTS_at_a_press_conference_for_the_BBMAs_(3).png

Tochanyeol (2014) EXO at Mnet Asian Music Awards in 2014. CC-by-4.0. https://ko.m.wikipedia.org/wiki/%ED%8C%8C%EC%9D%BC:Exo,_MAMA_2014.jpg

Yeh, Shannon (2012) Rice Donation by K-pop fans. CC-by-2.0. https://commons.wikimedia.org/wiki/File:Fan_rice_for_EXO.jpg

Yoon Min-hoo (2016) IU for Sony, 25 July 2016. CC-by-4.0 https://de.wikipedia.org/wiki/IU_(S%C3%A4ngerin)#/media/File:IU_for_Sony,_25_July_2016_04.jpg

Learn Korean Language with K-pop Song Lyrics! Volume 1, 2, & 3

by Annika Chung

1st Edition (2017)
2nd Edition (2018)

For more information, visit
www.coalharbourpublishing

22597754R00100

Made in the USA
San Bernardino, CA
15 January 2019